ck City Had Everton
Slide

ampions Everton were out-
street yesterday by a Leicester
erior than the 2-0 final score

Merseysiders reduced to pl
t England

T0294098

TER CI
L CLUB

SEAS
196
1964

TER CITY
v
ERTON

th DECEMBER 1963

LEAGUE
CHAMPIONS
1954-55

Chelsea
Football Club
Stamford Bridge Grounds, London SW6

FOOTBALL LEAGUE—DIVISION I

CHELSEA
v
BLACKPOOL

Saturday, 28th December, 1963

Programme   6D

Also available at all good book stores

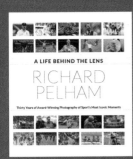

9781785315466

9781785313929

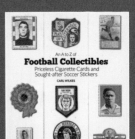

9781785315602

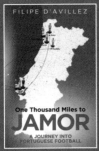

9781785316258

9781785316869

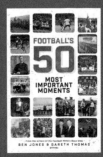

9781785316326

9781785316708

9781785315534

9781785316449

Late December Back in '63

Pitch Publishing Ltd
A2 Yeoman Gate
Yeoman Way
Durrington
BN13 3QZ

Email: info@pitchpublishing.co.uk
Web: www.pitchpublishing.co.uk

First published by Pitch Publishing 2020
Text © 2020 Ian Davidson

1

A CIP catalogue record for this book is available from the British Library.

13-digit ISBN: 9781785316845
Design and typesetting by Olner Pro Sport Media. Visit www.olnerpsm.com
Printed and bound in India by Replika Press Pvt. Ltd.

Late December Back in '63
The Boxing Day Goal Frenzy

IAN DAVIDSON

FIRST DIVISION – DECEMBER 26, 1963

Blackpool	1 - 5	Chelsea
Burnley	6 - 1	Manchester United
Fulham	10- 1	Ipswich Town
Leicester City	2 - 0	Everton
Liverpool	6 - 1	Stoke City
Nottingham Forest	3 - 3	Sheffield United
Sheffield Wednesday	3 - 0	Bolton Wanderers
West Bromwich Albion	4 - 4	Tottenham Hotspur
West Ham United	2 - 8	Blackburn Rovers
Wolves	3 - 3	Aston Villa

Index

Foreword

I can well remember the approach of late December back in '63 with much trepidation. A year earlier snow had started falling on Boxing Day and the temperatures stayed below freezing for weeks. It was arguably the worst winter of the 20th century. For a football-mad teenager the frustration seemed never ending, unable to play and no games to watch.

There was no undersoil heating then, though Leicester City earned the title of 'Ice Kings' thanks to an imaginative groundsman who laid down straw on their pitch and stayed up all night putting fuel on braziers. The Foxes managed to fulfil their home fixtures and might have won the league, but the consequent imbalance of away games towards the end of a season which was extended until June became too big a hurdle.

Happily, there was no repeat of that Siberian spell a year on. The programme of top-level football at that time in the football calendar has never before or since seemed so festive. My personal memory is of the two games between West Ham and Blackburn Rovers. The 2-8 scoreline on 26 December made huge headlines and the 3-1 reverse two days later probably spawned the cliché, which still exists today, that 'you get strange results over Christmas'.

A full programme of Football League fixtures on Christmas Day itself had only recently been discontinued. No public transport was the main reason, although all these years later fans manage to travel up and down the country on Boxing Day when trains and buses do not run. One other difference in the schedule concerned New Year's Day. It was not deemed a public holiday in England until the mid-70s, so the week leading up to the third round of the FA Cup on the first weekend in January was much freer for rest, recovery and preparation after the hectic schedule around Christmas.

One prevailing condition in 1963 was the wind, the wind of change. The maximum wage, a Football League salary cap, had been challenged in the courts by the Professional Footballers' Association and the players had won. Ties that had bound a footballer to a club for as long as that employer chose to keep him were also broken.

Tactically, there was more freedom too. New formations were being tried as the old 2-3-5 W-M system was being phased out. Managers who were often seen in trench coats and trilby hats now put on tracksuits. Kit was made of lighter material, particularly the boots and the ball.

By December 1963, Alf Ramsey was installed as manager of England and was embarking on a journey which would take England to lifting the World Cup. George Best had made his debut for Manchester United in the September and the first seeds of celebrity footballers were sown. The 60s had started to swing. Football has always reflected society and in my young mind at that time there was a great connection between the mood of the country and the national game.

At 18, in 1963, I was very innocent compared to that age group today and with hindsight I think football was too. The events of late December 1963 reflect that. Grinding out wins did not seem to be part of the culture, though that would soon change. Make no mistake, the bonuses for winning were still important for the top-level professionals, who were still essentially working-class men, but the scrutiny over results was far less intense.

In-depth analysis was on the way. Even Ramsey faced heavy criticism before the World Cup three years later, though he had the last laugh. Football was becoming much more pragmatic. No wingers for England after the group stage and in those six triumphant games the tournament winners scored only 11 goals, four of them in the final, and two of those in extra time.

In that context the extraordinary goal-crammed First Division games of late December 1963 do represent the end of an era. Those stories which have been exhumed for this excellent book richly deserve to be commemorated.

Read on...

Martin Tyler

Football Commentator Sky Sports

Introduction

Late December Back In '63 – The Day Football Went Crazy, gives you the inside story of one of the most dramatic days in the history of top-flight English football. On Boxing Day 1963, an incredible 66 goals were scored in the ten fixtures played and a host of club and personal records were broken, including:

- Record home win

- Record away win

- Record match aggregate

- Three players scored four goals

- Eight hat-tricks

- And one missed penalty

That day, 157 goals were scored across the whole Football League and the reasons why goals were plentiful will be examined, along with the characters who starred that day and the social and sports history prevalent at that time.

Furthermore, a chapter is dedicated to the players who won the World Cup for England only two and a half years later – read how their respective careers were developing and how the seeds of England's World Cup triumph of 1966 were being sown.

You will also read about the first goal of a future legend of the game – perhaps the best there has ever been. Can you guess who that could be?

But first of all, to give sport some context, let's set the scene as to what life was like in 1963. Enjoy this trip down Memory Lane!

On Boxing Day 1962 it rained and snowed heavily.

On Boxing Day 1963 it rained goals!

Chapter 1

Setting the Scene

Before we get stuck into the football on Boxing Day 1963, it is worth spending a few minutes wrapping some context around the day by exploring:

- the global and domestic scene

- the lot of the players in 1963

- the English First Division football structure

- the very limited media profile football had back then

I will also explore the theories as to why there were so many goals scored on this day, knocking down some of the myths and expanding on some of the more valid ones.

This is important for anyone born after 1990 who has grown up in a digital world where information and content goes around the world in an instant – 1963 was not like that as we shall see.

World and Domestic Events

The world had settled down to a period of peace, 18 years after the end of World War Two and one year after the Cuban Missile Crisis had threatened nuclear war.

There were some significant world events in 1963:

- the assassination of President Kennedy in November was one of those 'where were you' moments

- tensions in Vietnam had escalated, with 16,000 US 'advisors' now stationed in South Vietnam

- civil and economic rights for all were also on the world agenda, with Martin Luther King giving his 'I Have A Dream' speech in August 1963. A speech considered by many as one of the greatest orations of all time

It is chastening to acknowledge that even as recently as 1963, some of the world's population could not use certain facilities due to the colour of their skin – but that was soon to change in the USA, after King's assassination in 1968.

Domestic Landscape and UK Political Scene

Following the end of World War Two, economic recovery had been slow (rationing of certain products had only ended in 1954), but by the late 1950s the nation was enjoying something of a modest economic revival with almost full employment.

Industries such as steel, mining, housing and car production were flourishing (the Hillman Imp production facility in Scotland and the Ford Anglia facility in Merseyside both opened in 1963). Readers of a certain age will recall Prime Minister Macmillan's quote: 'You've never had it so good' in 1959.

However, 1963 was not all positive, with the beginning of the Moors Murders that would claim the lives of five young children in gruesome circumstances in the north of England. The Profumo Scandal rocked the political world, leading to the resignation of a Secretary of State after lying to Parliament and, indirectly, to a change of government in 1964.

1963 was also the year of the Great Train Robbery, when a train was audaciously hijacked in Buckinghamshire, with the perpetrators making off with a fortune, before the vast majority of the gang were caught. The robbery is still generally recognised as one of the most famous criminal acts in history.

How the robbery was reported in the press, and the huge sum of money offered as a reward by the Postmaster General.

Culture, Music & Fashion

With the ravages of World War Two finally becoming a distant memory, the UK started to get its mojo back, following the drab 1950s. If the 50s were dull and grey, then the 1960s were exciting and colourful. All types of culture were beginning to reflect individuality, including fashion, music, hairstyles, entertainment and food. It became acceptable once again to have an identity.

Music was a defining element of the early 60s. Rock 'n' Roll had started to have an effect from the late 1950s (for example Bill

Pos	LW		Title, Artist	
1	1		I WANT TO HOLD YOUR HAND THE BEATLES	PARLOPHONE
2	2		SHE LOVES YOU THE BEATLES	PARLOPHONE
3	3		YOU WERE MADE FOR ME FREDDIE AND THE DREAMERS	COLUMBIA
4	9↑		GLAD ALL OVER THE DAVE CLARK FIVE	COLUMBIA
5	4↓		SECRET LOVE KATHY KIRBY	DECCA
6	7↑		I ONLY WANT TO BE WITH YOU DUSTY SPRINGFIELD	PHILIPS
7	5↓		MARIA ELENA LOS INDIOS TABAJARAS	RCA
8	10↑		DOMINIQUE THE SINGING NUN	PHILIPS
9	20↑		TWENTY FOUR HOURS FROM TULSA GENE PITNEY	UNITED ARTISTS
10	6↓		DON'T TALK TO HIM CLIFF RICHARD	COLUMBIA

The Top Ten in December 1963.

Haley), but it was not until 1963, with the emergence of The Beatles and The Rolling Stones, amongst many others, that music really began to change and influence the lives of young people. The Beatles released 'I Want To Hold Your Hand' as a single and their first album *Please Please Me* in March 1963. Music would never be the same again.

In fashion, Carnaby Street and similar areas in cities throughout the UK became central to new ways of dressing and became beacons of change in their field. The country started to feel good about itself again and a new fashion culture was developing.

The average wage for a skilled worker in 1963 was about £18 to £20 per week, with the working week lasting 45 hours, including Saturday mornings ... just enough time left to attend a football match! Rent and housing costs were also modest (a house would cost between £1,500 and £2,500, with rent at approximately £4 per week). Most people, especially the young, had surplus funds to invest in looking good and having a good time.

This movement was aided by the abolition of National Service during the three-year period 1960 to 1963 (the last call-ups were December 1960 and the last servicemen left in May 1963). Almost all of the players who played in the 1963 Boxing Day fixtures served Queen & Country at some stage, and National Service had a major impact on many of their football careers, putting it on hold for two years.

This was the first 'free' generation whose parents had likely served in a world war and they set out to enjoy themselves with their new freedoms. Young people finally had the opportunity to do what they wanted, with whom they wanted. And they were encouraged to do so by their parents, as they had spent their youth with war hanging over them.

Popular destinations included cinemas, coffee shops, Wimpy bars, snooker halls (mainly for the boys), dance halls and record shops, where you could gather with your friends to listen to the latest single releases in the play booths – probably first heard on Radio Luxembourg 208 (BBC Radio One was still four years away).

In many ways the early 60s was a defining period for popular culture in the UK – full of optimism, hope and promise for the future. It became known as the 'Swinging Sixties' and spawned a generation who began to stand up for their beliefs and individuality.

I will let the reader decide whether that was a good thing or bad!

Climate Issues

The previous winter of 1962–63 was one of the worst winters on record. Becoming known as 'The Big Freeze', it severely disrupted the football calendar, with the FA Cup third round taking months to complete. The average temperature in January 1963 was -2.1°C, which remains the coldest month since January 1814.

There was very heavy snow on Boxing Day 1962, followed by blizzards on 29 and 30 December, and snow continued to fall throughout January and February 1963. It wasn't until 6 March that the UK enjoyed a frost-free day, such was the severity of the winter. Taken as a three-month period, only the winters of 1683–84 and 1839–40 were colder than 1962–63.

Some football fixtures were rescheduled ten times or more, causing some clubs to suffer cash flow problems, such was their reliance on gate income. The repeated postponements caused the formation of the 'Pools Panel' to decide results of fixtures so that Pools companies could continue to function.

Eventually, thanks to a four-week extension to the season to mid-May, all league fixtures were completed the day before the rescheduled FA Cup Final (between Manchester United and Leicester City). Although the professional leagues completed their seasons, many junior leagues up and down the country did not.

The following winter of 1963–64, although very cold, was fortunately not as harsh; however, the wintry conditions still played their part on the festive programme. One of the casualties of the previous season's fixtures was the postponement of the whole Boxing Day programme and the effects of this became one of the possible reasons why there were so many goals in the 1963 games.

A dogged postman fights the snow drifts, to deliver his letters in January 1963.

The Players

Throughout most of the late 1950s, players were paid on average £17 to £18 per week. Wages were strictly controlled but small incentives could help – £4 for a win and £2 for a draw, with extra bonuses if the attendances exceeded a certain level, were often written into contracts.

By 1959 the maximum wage stipulated by the Football League was £20 per week, but by the end of the decade the Professional Footballers' Association – led by ex-player, future manager and pundit Jimmy Hill – threatened a strike if that ceiling was not lifted. Towards the end of January 1961, the footballing authorities finally relented, allowing clubs to pay whatever they wanted to their employees, like any other company.

England international Johnny Haynes of Fulham became the first high-profile recipient, earning £100 per week, but in reality he was a rarity and his wage remained at that level for the next eight years of his playing career. Alan Mullery, who shared a dressing room with Haynes during his time at Fulham, quoted that all the players were excited by Haynes's huge pay rise, but in reality the majority of other players, including Mullery, received a rise of just £8 – from £20 to £28; still welcomed but hardly a fortune. Johnny Byrne, an international player when he signed for West Ham United in 1962, received £40 per week – a decent wage back then, but nowhere near the riches that players earn following satellite TV investment in the early 90s.

As well as the maximum wage, players had to contend with the 'retain-and-transfer' system. Essentially, once a player signed for a club he lost his right to a transfer from them, as the club now 'owned' him, resulting in the player losing his right to change employer of his own free will.

This was challenged by an established Newcastle United player, George Eastham, who requested a transfer as his contract neared its end in 1959. His club refused to let him go, so Eastham moved to London and worked in an office in Surrey until the situation was resolved. Newcastle were ultimately found guilty by Lord Justice Wilberforce of 'restraint of trade' as Eastham was 'denied rights extended to other trades and professions'. As a result, the employment and movement of footballers changed from that point forward. Eastham eventually joined Arsenal for £47,500 to continue his successful career.

This court ruling did, however, increase the opportunities for clubs to 'tap up' players they wanted to sign. Frank McLintock (one of the best young players in the country at that time) indicated in his book that, whilst at Leicester, the Leeds United manager Don Revie arrived at his door one evening offering him £60 per week and £8,000 in cash (about three times the value of an average house) to sign for the Yorkshire club. McLintock's wage at that time was just £30 (having only just received an increase from £15 per week) and, as such, he was very tempted by Revie's offer, but out of loyalty to the Leicester City board and manager Matt Gillies, he turned it down – which proved a tad awkward as Matt Gillies and Don Revie had a good relationship!

Although terms and conditions for footballers were improving slowly in 1963, their careers rarely lasted until their mid-30s, due to their diets and lack of conditioning coaching. Lifestyles in this era often involved excess alcohol, inappropriate diets and late nights, resulting in injuries as a result of strained, tired bodies. Johnny Byrne, who is featured later in this book, admitted in his biography that, 'he liked the booze too much' and that he was past his best as a First Division and international footballer by the age of 29.

The diagnosis and treatment of bad injuries were also a contributory factor to the length of a footballer's career, as methods of rehabilitation were very basic by modern standards. As such, injuries like leg breaks, cartilage and ligament damage would often end a career prematurely.

Many footballers lived in the local community, often in the same terraced streets as the fans. As a result, they would often eat and drink in the same pubs, clubs and cafés too. Furthermore, they frequently travelled to home fixtures on the same buses as fans, they just entered the ground for free and through a different gate!

This was also the era when many more players (not all) were servants of just one club, as the financial benefits of moving on were not as apparent as in the modern world. In the 1960s and 1970s players who served ten years often qualified for a testimonial, which very often provided an adequate financial reward to set them up after their playing days with a business such as a pub or a newsagent.

Every footballer you are about to read about needed to work after they finished playing, whether that was within the game or not, as very few were able to be effective on the pitch past their 32nd birthday.

National Football Landscape

The National team did not enjoy a successful decade in the 1950s, bizarrely losing 1-0 to then minnows USA in the 1950 World Cup and then in 1953 and 1954 being taken apart 6-3 (at Wembley) and 7-1 (in Budapest) by the amazing Hungarian team of that period, thus ending a period of English superiority at Wembley.

Additionally, England failed at the 1958 World Cup in Sweden (when all four home nations qualified for the finals for the first and only time), by drawing all three group matches and being eliminated at the first hurdle. Their cause was, of course, not helped by the Munich tragedy in March 1958, when many of the outstanding crop of young footballers developed by Manchester United perished on the way home from a European Cup semi-final, including the majestic Duncan Edwards who was widely recognised as the finest player of his generation and destined to become one of the all-time greats.

The First Division Structure 1963/64

It was a lop-sided and clustered First Division in 1963/64, reflecting the football power-houses of that era and the division was, geographically, split into three.

Firstly the 'old Lancashire' (before county boundaries changed) boasted seven clubs from the towns of Burnley, Blackburn, Blackpool and Bolton, backed up by city clubs Liverpool, Everton and Manchester United. It's worth noting that Liverpool, under Bill Shankly, had only just been promoted from Division Two, whilst Manchester City were still in the second tier (they put eight past Scunthorpe that day).

All seven clubs were within easy travelling distance of each other and a healthy rivalry existed between them. However, it is no surprise that the four town clubs have all struggled in more recent times, as big city revenues developed and increased. All four have spent time in the bottom two leagues, with Burnley almost going out of the Football League altogether in 1986, before beginning the long climb back up to the top flight, where they are situated today. A great achievement for a town of just 73,000 inhabitants.

These four relatively small Lancashire clubs were able to sustain long periods of time in the top flight, due partly to the maximum wage, as players would only receive the same £20 per week (and sometimes not even that) regardless of whether they played for a small-town club or a big-city club. However, the lifting of the maximum wage was the start of a very slow, but very evident, decline of small-town clubs in the top flight of English football, as eventually over time the larger, wealthier city clubs gained the upper hand, as they could pay higher wages.

The next geographic cluster was across the Pennines in Yorkshire, as both Sheffield clubs were represented in the First Division. Note the absence of Leeds United, although they were busy getting promoted from Division Two under Don Revie and would go on to become a power-house for just over a decade. In addition, it should be noted that none of the big three north-eastern clubs were in Division One, although Sunderland were to join Leeds in getting promotion in 1963/64.

Coming further south, the West Midlands were represented by four clubs all within a ten-mile radius – Aston Villa, their second-city colleagues Birmingham City and their Black Country rivals West Bromwich Albion and Wolverhampton Wanderers, creating much interest in that part of the world. Also in the Midlands, but in the east, were Nottingham Forest and Leicester City, whilst Stoke in the north made up a very healthy Midlands football scene of seven.

The final significant cluster was obviously in London, although bizarrely none were south of the river. Representing North London were Arsenal and Tottenham Hotspur, who have a long standing ambivalence towards each other, after Arsenal's relocation from south-of-the-river Woolwich to Highbury in North London in the early 20th century. West Ham United represented the East London community, with the west represented by two clubs just two miles apart, Chelsea and Fulham.

The final club to make up the division was Ipswich Town, who were in easy reach of North and East London along the A12.

The strange geographical quirk of the top flight that season saw no teams from the south-west, none in South London, none from the south coast, and none in the North East, which made for a congested championship in the traditional footballing regions, although this would slowly change throughout the 1970s and 1980s.

Press and Media Coverage

With the first *Match of the Day* still 12 months away and two years before it occupied a prime slot on BBC One, there was limited broadcast media profile for football in 1963, despite mass interest and high attendances – nearly 13 million fans attended First Division fixtures in 1963/64.

Match of the Day was not originally universally welcomed and several clubs tried to block it in 1965, fearing that it may affect attendances. To placate clubs, the BBC had to agree to a deal whereby they would not reveal the fixture televised, until after the day's play was concluded. Early audiences were poor with less than 30,000 tuning in to some of the initial episodes on BBC2.

Football fans and casual followers alike relied upon newspapers, radio, match programmes and magazines such as *Charles Buchan's Football Monthly*, which gave readers images of the stars that they had heard of on the radio.

The *Charles Buchan's Football Monthly* magazine was very popular in its day.

The radio offered *Sports Report* (still running at 5pm every Saturday, with its iconic music), which was an essential listen, as it rounded up the scores of the day. In December 1963 it was hosted by Irishman Eamonn Andrews and went out on the BBC Light Programme before moving to the BBC Third Programme a short time later.

Of particular interest was the *Saturday Evening Sports Special* newspapers, which were printed very soon after the final whistles blew up and down the country. They were then distributed quickly to city-centre street vendors, where a gaggle of expectant folk were waiting to read all about that day's fixtures. With all games kicking off on Saturday at 3pm, readers could see where that left their club in the league table.

These editions were highly popular in big cities and often printed in a different colour to differentiate themselves from the normal daily paper – e.g. in Sheffield it was called the *Green 'Un*, in Leicester it was *The Buff*, whilst in Manchester it was the *Sporting Pink*. It was a remarkable logistical exercise, although the match content was necessarily basic as speed was of the essence, with copies often hitting the High Street just an hour after the games had ended. It is interesting to note that the pink shirt worn by Manchester United in 2018 was dedicated to the demise of the *Sporting Pink*.

Despite there being no internet, Ceefax or even universal ownership of televisions, the enduring appeal of the sport was strong and was soon to grow even stronger with the introduction of regular, recorded football on the BBC, in the form of *Match of the Day*. It began in 1964 on BBC Two, showed just one fixture and was originally presented by Kenneth Wolstenholme. By the time of the 1966 World Cup, all fixtures were televised and England's success was embraced by the nation.

These two developments brought new audiences to the sport and the stars became much more visually accessible. However, just two decades later, the sad spectre of hooliganism and poor in-ground facilities meant that growth was stilted, until the development of the Premier League in 1992, which brought with it investment in stadia and an emerging, more discerning clientele.

Why So Many Goals?

It was not only the First Division that saw goals aplenty that day. There were 157 goals scored across all four divisions – approximately four goals per game – with Manchester City leading the way outside Division One by thrashing Scunthorpe 8-1 in Division Two. There was just one goalless draw across the four divisions, with Crewe Alexandra and Peterborough United from Division Three being the unwitting culprits.

The reasons for the number of goals that day, especially in the top flight, make for an interesting debate, with many justifications being put forward in subsequent years:

- Fatigue due to a hectic December fixture schedule

- Fatigue due to excessive travelling

- Excessive Christmas celebrations

- Making up for no Boxing Day fixtures the previous season

- Freak weather conditions and poor pitches, making it difficult for defenders

- An attacking philosophy being the 'norm' at that time

Fatigue due to the Christmas schedule

The allegation of fatigue due to players perhaps playing football on consecutive days is false, as there were no fixtures played on Christmas Day. With Boxing Day falling on a Thursday, the holiday fixtures were scheduled for Saturday/Thursday/Saturday, thus giving players five days' rest before playing on Boxing Day. We can therefore dismiss fatigue as a mitigation.

Christmas Day fixtures were popular for a while (the last full programme was in 1957) but became less so with fans as they found travel difficult due to a lack of public transport. Moreover, the menfolk would almost certainly be pressured into spending Christmas Day at home with their family – pressure that your author faced on a regular basis and continues to do so today!

The last Christmas Day First Division fixture was in 1965 – Blackpool versus Blackburn. The Seasiders kept the fixture going longer than most as the town would attract thousands of visitors at Christmas, driving up the gate for the match, which would often sell out.

Fatigue due to excessive travelling

The second possibility offered, of fatigue due to travelling, can also be discounted, as only Blackburn, who travelled to East London to play West Ham United, and Chelsea, who travelled to the north-west coast to play Blackpool, had significant trips that would have definitively required overnight stays. Chelsea travelled on Christmas Eve due to the lack of trains on Christmas Day, whilst Blackburn travelled on Christmas Day, as their Boxing Day game kicked off at 11am, so an overnight stay was essential.

All the other fixtures required acceptable travelling time on match day itself – with the fixtures at Burnley (v Manchester United), Fulham (v Ipswich), Liverpool (v Stoke), Nottingham Forest (v Sheffield United), Sheffield Wednesday (v Bolton) and Wolves (v Aston Villa) being fairly short trips for the away side.

Excessive Christmas celebrations

It is also unlikely, although not impossible, that excessive seasonal celebrations played their part in this collection of crazy results. Almost all of the participating players, interviewed after their games, denied that excessive partying was a factor, with the vast majority of players enjoying a night at their homes before travelling to their respective fixtures. It is possible, of course, that one or two players did drink and eat to excess, as there were several 'characters' amongst them; however, my hunch is that this factor was not particularly significant.

No Boxing Day fixtures the previous season

A fourth possible explanation that's been touted is that players were 'making up' for the previous season's Boxing Day fixtures, which were nearly all wiped out due to snow. However, this is highly unlikely as players focus and plan for the forthcoming fixture without worrying about past postponements.

Although players did enjoy Boxing Day games, as they nearly always attracted larger crowds and had a holiday feel about them, the fact that they had lost the equivalent fixture the previous year would, in my opinion, have had no bearing on the results in 1963.

Freak weather conditions & poor pitches

There had been five days of freezing temperatures immediately prior to Christmas, followed by a quick thaw. Rain then fell, causing the top surface on many pitches to form a slimy layer upon a frozen crust – most particularly at West Ham, Leicester, Fulham and West Bromwich.

These conditions, slippery but playable, made defending difficult and attackers were able to capitalise as defenders couldn't turn quickly. The conditions, therefore, were certainly a factor in the day's play.

An attacking philosophy being the 'norm' at that time

The sixth possible reason is certainly true, as over the whole season in Division One there were 1,571 goals scored in 462 fixtures – an average of 3.4 goals per game. Furthermore, five players scored 30 or more goals that season – an extremely rare event. By way of comparison, the modern Premier League averages 2.8 goals per game.

Therefore, attackers were, generally speaking, getting the better of defenders, as it was the era before improved defensive discipline, brought on eventually by, in part, English teams playing in Europe. This was soon to change, however, as tactics became a little more sophisticated throughout the rest of the decade, epitomised by Alf Ramsey's World Cup winning England team of 1966, who played without traditional touchline-hugging wingers.

The First Half of Season 1963/1964

The 1960s was an interesting decade for First Division football as it was the last time when there was a discernible footballing equality, with eight different clubs winning the First Division championship – a record for a single decade and unlikely to be repeated. This list included small town, provincial clubs, Burnley and Ipswich Town, as they could assemble, and keep, a competitive team reasonably cheaply. It was also possible to develop and retain outstanding youth players, unlike in the modern game where promising young players often leave after just one season.

The season began with Everton defending their title and participating in the European Cup. Newly promoted Chelsea and Stoke City looked to establish themselves back amongst the elite, and, although Chelsea were predicted to do well, Stoke City were expected to struggle. Arsenal and Sheffield Wednesday took part in the Inter Cities Fairs Cup, whilst Manchester United were in the European Cup Winners' Cup.

It was generally felt that the First Division championship race would be an open one, with no outstanding candidates. As well as champions Everton, Tottenham (who had won the European Cup Winners' Cup in 1962/63) looked strong, whilst Liverpool and Manchester United were developing excellent young teams under iconic managers Bill Shankly and Matt Busby.

Initial thoughts amongst fans centred on the forthcoming winter, hoping that it wouldn't be as harsh as the previous one, and towards the 1966 World Cup, now just three seasons away.

The season kicked off on 17 August with the traditional curtain raiser, the Charity Shield held at Goodison Park. Not surprisingly, reigning champions Everton beat FA Cup winners Manchester United 4-0.

There were some high-scoring fixtures in the first couple of months, with Arsenal leading the way beating Ipswich 6-0, Bolton 4-3, and Fulham 4-1, whilst losing 7-2 at Leicester. These were followed by a 4-4 draw in the North London derby, with almost 68,000 present at Highbury on 15 October. Liverpool had a bizarre start, losing their first three home fixtures but winning three out of their first four away fixtures. They too were involved in some high-scoring games, putting six past Wolves and five past Aston Villa.

On 14 September a future legend of British football made his first-team debut, when a 17-year-old George Best was selected to play for Manchester United versus West Bromwich Albion at Old Trafford, with United winning 1-0. However, Best had to wait until the Christmas period to play again.

At the end of September, most teams had played ten fixtures and the top of the table was incredibly tight, with five teams on 14 points – Manchester United, West Brom, Spurs, Sheffield United and Nottingham Forest. Blackburn were only one point further back, with Arsenal in seventh and champions-to-be Liverpool in eighth, both on 11 points.

By the end of November, with most teams having played 21 fixtures – halfway through the programme – Liverpool had developed more consistency and were top, but only on goal difference from a rapidly emerging Blackburn, who were on a great run which was to continue up until Boxing Day. Spurs, Arsenal and Manchester United made up the top five, Everton sat in seventh, whilst Chelsea sat in mid-table.

Ipswich, sadly, had only won one fixture at this point, having already conceded 53 goals, and were bottom of the league with just six points – and it was to get even worse for them. They had been champions only 18 months previously but had lost Alf Ramsey to the England job. Bolton joined them in the bottom two and their 30-year stay in the First Division was in serious danger.

The top of the table clash at Anfield on 14 December was won by Blackburn, thanks to two goals from Andy McEvoy, taking them to the summit. As the Boxing Day fixtures loomed large, the top of the table was thus:

Pos.		P	W	D	L	F	A	Pts	GA
1st	Blackburn	24	13	6	5	52	29	32	1.793
2nd	Tottenham	22	14	4	4	61	39	32	1.564
3rd	Liverpool	22	14	2	6	40	22	30	1.818
4th	Arsenal	25	12	5	8	65	52	29	1.250
5th	Man. United	23	12	4	7	46	32	28	1.438
6th	Everton	23	11	6	6	42	36	28	1.167

Ipswich Town and Bolton Wanderers occupied the two relegation spots, which at Christmas time is, in most cases, an accurate barometer as to who would eventually go down … and they both did.

As working-class fans up and down the country paid their six shillings (30p post-decimalisation – equivalent to £5 today) for entrance into their respective clubs, little were they to know that the First Division would go goal crazy.

———

So, the scene is set. Sit back and enjoy the story of one of the most remarkable days of English league football that there has ever been. Get to know some of the many, varied characters who helped make the day so special – a snapshot of an incredible day in football history.

We start off with an amazing fixture in the East End of London, at Upton Park, the home of West Ham United – the only fixture to start at 11am. Many journalists from the national press were present as opponents Blackburn Rovers were in great form and leading the First Division.

In reality, however, they attended in order that they could return to Fleet Street by the early afternoon, file their copy, and return home shortly after 5pm to enjoy the rest of their Boxing Day.

They certainly had a morning to remember.

WEST HAM UNITED

BLACKBURN ROVERS

FOOTBALL LEAGUE—Division One

THURSDAY 26th DECEMBER 1963 at 11 a.m.

No. 31

The Directors, Players and Staff
of the West Ham United Football Club
extend Heartiest Seasonal Greetings
to all their friends in the Realm of
Soccer both "at Home and Away"

OFFICIAL PROGRAMME 6ᵈ

Balliar & Sons, London. E.13

CDEFGHIJKL

Chapter 2

West Ham United v Blackburn Rovers

2 - 8

Kick-off: 11am   **Venue: Upton Park**   **Attendance: 34,500**

Standen	1	Else
Bond	2	Bray
Burkett	3	Newton
Peters	4	Clayton
Brown	5	England
Moore	6	McGrath
Brabrook	7	Ferguson ⚽
Boyce	8	McEvoy ⚽⚽⚽
⚽⚽ Byrne	9	Pickering ⚽⚽⚽
Hurst	10	Douglas ⚽
Sissons	11	Harrison

The Managers
Ron Greenwood   Jack Marshall

Match Report

The Upton Park clash kicked off at 11am and started Boxing Day proceedings in spectacular style with ten goals ... and all before lunch!

East End football fans rose early that morning and made their way to their spiritual home Upton Park in their thousands. Off at Upton Park Tube, turn right out of the station and walk a few hundred yards past the jellied eels and pie 'n' mash stalls and into the atmospheric and much lamented Upton Park.

At this time, Blackburn Rovers and West Ham United had a healthy and respectful rivalry, the seeds of which were sown in the 1959 FA Youth Cup Final, which Blackburn Rovers shaded 2-1 over two legs (after extra time). Over 10,000 were at Upton Park for the first leg, whilst a mammoth 28,500 attended the second leg at Ewood Park, with both teams being presented to FIFA dignitary Stanley Rous.

West Ham United youth team 1959, featuring Bobby Moore (far right, back row). Moore captained the team and looked a football colossus even at 18. Geoff Hurst also featured but in the second leg only.

Five of the participants in this Boxing Day clash played in that Youth Cup Final, including future West Ham and England legend Bobby Moore and Blackburn Rovers' future star striker Fred Pickering, who at that time was a full-back and captain of Blackburn Youth.

Blackburn Rovers were a reasonably successful club in the early 60s, with some excellent footballers on their books, finishing eighth in Division One in season 1960/61, whilst the season before they reached the FA Cup Final, but lost 3-0 to Wolves after losing a player – Dave Whelan – to a broken leg in the pre-substitute days. Whelan went on to become a successful businessman and owner of Wigan Athletic.

West Ham United were developing a fine side too at this point in their history and were on the cusp of some long overdue silverware. They had an effective youth policy that started to produce some excellent footballers, that continues to this day.

However, West Ham went into their home Boxing Day fixture in the bottom third of the table, after only six wins in the opening 23 league fixtures and no win since 2 November. By contrast, Blackburn were in hot form – unbeaten in 11, and top of the First Division at the start of the Christmas programme.

But the league leaders' preparations for the fixture were not ideal, as Rovers' Fred Pickering recounted many years later. They had an awful journey to Upton Park as they travelled by train on Christmas Day, via Preston with no food available on the train – and with no food upon arrival at Euston Station and no food available at their London hotel either, their pre-match eating itinerary was in disarray. The league's top team were in danger of going to bed on an empty stomach before an important First Division fixture!

However, one of the junior players came to the rescue when he successfully found an open fish and chip shop (on Christmas Day!) and the players duly got fed. Up early for breakfast, and with no hotel staff around, the players ate lightly (toast) before heading over to Upton Park by 10am – not ideal preparation for athletes in a top flight fixture but it didn't seem to affect their performance too much!

There was a strange playing surface at Upton Park that morning. The pitch was without doubt playable but after several days of frost there was a quick surface thaw, followed by some heavy rain that left the

The imperious Bryan Douglas scoring for Blackburn Rovers in the mud at Upton Park to put Blackburn Rovers 2-1 up on the half-hour mark. The stand in the background was the 'Chicken Run' whose patrons were some of the most humorous in the league.

surface 'slimy' but slick in places. As a result, players found it difficult to turn quickly.

The fixture started that morning with 34,500 present and it was immediately obvious that in-form Blackburn were up for a contest. They moved the ball quickly and effectively, with the majestic Bryan Douglas (slight of frame but big on passing talent) leading the Hammers a merry dance in midfield, revelling in the freedom offered by the opposition.

Fred 'Boomer' Pickering opened the scoring for Blackburn after just six minutes from 20 yards out, with a typical strong shot but Johnny 'Budgie' Byrne's equaliser five minutes later was even more impressive as he turned and swivelled past three Rovers defenders before bending the ball around a transfixed Fred Else in the Blackburn goal.

Shortly after, Byrne almost put the Hammers ahead but his shot struck the crossbar. Bryan Douglas then restored Blackburn's lead on 30 minutes, slipping the ball under Jim Standen after a fine passing move had opened up the West Ham defence.

Blackburn then really turned on the style and goals by Andy McEvoy and Mike Ferguson secured Rovers a 4-1 lead at half-time. The second half followed in a similar pattern and 10 minutes after the break, Pickering added his second with the Hammers defence 'wide open', according to press reports of the day.

Rovers did not have it all their own way though, and the irrepressible Byrne scored on the hour to just about keep the Hammers alive at 2-5. However, McEvoy's second five minutes later, settled the destination of the points, although a thunderbolt by Byrne on 72 minutes threatened to reduce the deficit once more, but his shot rattled the post. With just 18 minutes to go there was still enough time for McEvoy and Pickering to complete their hat-tricks, to give the scoreline a lop-sided look.

Although Blackburn were seriously impressive, they were perhaps not six goals better – it could easily have been 5-9 as West Ham missed a number of presentable chances, with Geoff Hurst in particular having an off-day.

Above and below: Andy McEvoy scoring two of his three for Blackburn Rovers.

Above: Hammers keeper Jim Standen looks despondent in the mud at Upton Park, as he conceded eight, despite making a few good saves.

EVEN THE HAMMERS' FANS HAD TO CHEER

West Ham 2, Blackburn 8

BLACKBURN, mud-caked and magnificent, squelched their way off the Upton Park pitch yesterday to a chorus of Cockney cheers, writes Harry Miller.

suffered their heaviest-ever home defeat.

Their tactics were all wrong and

find room for him on this form— scored after thirty minutes. Andy McEwan and Mike Ferguson

Douglas hands Moore misery

West Ham 2   Blackburn 8

WEST HAM'S saddened thousands and goalkeeper Jim Standen stood at the end to thunder applause for the men who had exploded the peace-and-plenty calm of Dockland, writes CLIVE TOYE.

It was a magnificent and deeply-felt tribute to Blackburn's unshakable defence and five-tongued menace in attack.

THE BLEND was in every swift move that left West Ham labouring in the mud.

THE CRAFT was in every limb but particularly in the tiny limbs of Bryan Douglas.

THE COURAGE was in the way Douglas and the four forwards he so-subtly promoted went into the tackles, went through the tackles and headed for goal.

It helped that West Ham were so poorly served at wing half by England's Bobby Moore and Young England's Martin Peters.

Rarely can two wing halves of their standing been found so often in the wrong place at the wrong time. Even rarer would be the admissions from wing halves that THEY had been tackled by tiny Douglas and lost the ball.

Five minutes from the start Fred Pickering scored the first goal. A minute from the end he scored the eighth.

And in between was some of the most glorious attacking football I could ever wish to see.

Johnny Byrne scored West Ham's two in the 10th and 40th minutes, Blackburn filled up their eight like this: Pickering (5, 52, 89), Andy McEvoy (25, 60, 78), Douglas (29), Mike Ferguson (40).

Blackburn left the field to well-deserved applause from the West Ham fans, in recognition that they had witnessed something very special indeed, with two away team hat-tricks to remember. Clive Toye in the *Daily Express* called it a 'deeply felt tribute' to the Lancastrian team.

Johnny Byrne's contribution for the Hammers must also not be forgotten. He was, at that time, England's centre-forward, and scored two goals whilst hitting the woodwork twice – he could have easily scored four that day, to add to the drama, and was in brilliant form.

The general consensus after the game was that West Ham had persisted with their short, crisp passing style despite it being totally unsuitable for the conditions. Furthermore, at least three of their players had off-days: Martin Peters, who lost control of Douglas numerous times, Geoff Hurst who, as mentioned earlier, missed some chances and winger Peter Brabrook who just couldn't adapt his game to the testing conditions.

Clive Toye's damning verdict on West Ham's performance, with future World Cup-winning stars Bobby Moore and Martin Peters lambasted for their positional and general play. Toye would go on to manage the New York Cosmos in the North American Soccer League and would famously sign Pele.

THERE was a distinct air of faint bewilderment about the Blackburn players at the end of this fantastic Boxing Day pantomime at Upton Park. One or two grabbed each other's hands in extra firm grips . . . . almost

WEST HAM UTD. 2
BLACKBURN R. 8

tional reasons for the debacle.
  The primary one possibly was the poor form of the injury-dogged Martin Peters, Hammers' Young England wing-half.
  Peter's failure allowed the elusive Douglas to enjoy a field

Blackburn forward Fred Pickering later commented that, 'It was just one of those games when everything we hit went in.'

The final score was a very rare occurrence indeed, with an away team scoring eight goals in the top flight of English football – a feat that's occurred just twice in the 27 years of the Premier League, when Manchester United won 8-1 at Nottingham Forest in 1999, and Leicester hit nine at Southampton in 2019.

It is also very rare that an away team scores two hat-tricks in a single fixture, but it happened on this day and has become one of the most memorable away wins in First Division history.

The result also set the following records:

• West Ham's heaviest home defeat

• Blackburn's greatest away win

• The best away win of the 1963/64 season

As the score and the copy was wired across London to all of the big daily newspapers and sports and news agencies alike, eyebrows were raised at the magnitude of the win. Little did everyone know, however, that this fixture was not even destined to be the highest win or the highest aggregate score of the day, never mind the season!

Blackburn stayed top after the fixture, but would soon fade away, ending the season in seventh position, whilst West Ham remained in a lowly 15th position (ending the season in 14th).

However, the Hammers would soon embark on a memorable FA Cup run – a run that would take them all the way to Wembley, whereupon they beat Preston North End 3-2 to lift the famous trophy for the first time in their history.

Return Match

 **Blackburn Rovers
1-3
West Ham United**

Date: 28 December   **Venue:** Ewood Park   **Att:** 28,890

With Blackburn having consolidated their position at the top of the table after thrashing West Ham at Upton Park, the return fixture 48 hours later was equally bizarre.

West Ham manager Ron Greenwood contemplated changes as he travelled north with, coincidentally, the Blackburn squad, as both teams shared the same train. A 16-year-old Harry Redknapp recalls hanging around Upton Park after the fixture in case he, or any of the Hammers youth team, were required for the trip north that afternoon, bearing in mind the result on Boxing Day.

In his autobiography, Johnny Byrne recalls that the team had a candid and honest team meeting in the hotel in Blackburn that evening, and all agreed that the Boxing Day performance had not been good enough. They were all determined to do something about it and he offers the view that all 11 could have been dropped with some justification.

However, manager Greenwood didn't panic after such a heavy home defeat, making just one change, dropping Martin Peters and replacing him with 'hard-man' Eddie Bovington.

Eddie was a great tackler and was given the job of drawing in the full-backs, forcing play out wide and man-marking Bryan Douglas, to stop the supply chain to Pickering and McEvoy.

The plan worked really well and on a sodden, rain-lashed pitch, West Ham turned the tables, winning 3-1 and handing Rovers their first defeat in 12 fixtures. However, Blackburn retained top spot as the New Year beckoned. Johnny Byrne scored twice at Ewood Park, having also scored twice at Upton Park, and there was, of course, another Rovers goal for the prolific McEvoy.

Very sadly for them, Blackburn were off the top of the table by mid-January and faded badly thereafter, ending the season seventh in the table, after winning just four of their remaining 18 league fixtures. Their season was hindered by losing Fred Pickering to Everton in March, and missing McEvoy for five fixtures in March/April, in which Rovers gained just one point.

This talented Rovers team declined still further by being relegated in 1966, and, just five years later, were relegated once again to Division Three. Not until the takeover by long-term fan Jack Walker in 1991 did Blackburn begin to recover, as his investment helped assemble a team that won promotion to the Premier League upon its inception in 1992 and memorably went on to win the Premier League in 1994/95.

Conversely, this return fixture was also the turning point for West Ham's season. With a defensively sound team (the blip on Boxing Day was the only time that they shipped more than three goals all season), they found success after Christmas, venturing on a great cup run that took them to their first Wembley FA Cup final since the 'White Horse' final of 1923.

They beat Preston North End 3-2 that day and followed that up 12 months later by beating 1860 Munich 2-0 in the final of the European Cup Winners' Cup at Wembley. And, of course, three of the side – Moore, Peters and Hurst – made it a hat-trick of Wembley wins a year later, starring for England in the 1966 World Cup Final.

It could easily be argued that that Boxing Day 8-2 victory was as good as it got for Blackburn Rovers in that era and as bad as it got for West Ham United as their paths diverged at that point, as so often happens.

West Ham, above, FA Cup winners in 1964 ...
        ... and, below, European Cup Winners' Cup winners in 1965.

PLAYER PROFILE
Frederick Pickering

Born in Blackburn on 19 January 1941, Fred signed professional forms with his home-town club on his 17th birthday, after being an apprentice at British Northrop. He was initially a defender of some promise and captained Blackburn in the 1959 Youth Cup Final as a full-back.

Fred made his debut versus Leicester City in October 1959, making a further three senior experiences during the season. It was not until the following season, however, that he had a more prolonged run in the team, following injuries to team-mates Whelan and Eckersley. But he soon returned to the backwaters of reserve-team football in the Central League, and at that stage his career looked to be stalling somewhat.

Manager Jack Marshall experimented by playing Fred as a centre-forward, and after scoring a Central League hat-trick versus Newcastle in March 1961 he earned a recall to the first team, scoring twice in a First Division game versus Manchester City in a 4-1 win. That performance kept him in the line-up for the rest of the season and it looked like Fred had found a new role.

Following six more goals in season 1961/62, he fully matured as a First Division striker in 1962/63, scoring 23 goals in 36 league fixtures, benefitting hugely from the supply provided by the graceful Bryan Douglas. In 1963/64 he found the perfect foil in Andy McEvoy and the pair complemented each other perfectly with their respective qualities. With Douglas supplying chances from midfield, the pair notched a glut of goals as Rovers mounted a serious title challenge, topping the league going into 1964.

However, in the spring of 1964 Pickering became restless, wanting to maximise his earnings as, by then, he was in England contention. He was being watched closely by Everton manager Harry Catterick, who'd been impressed when Fred scored a hat-trick against Everton in November 1963, helping Rovers win a bad-tempered fixture 4-2 at Goodison Park.

After scoring a brace in the 5-0 win for Rovers at Bolton on 29 February 1964, Pickering submitted a transfer request, which he made public, incurring a £25 fine. His request was approved by the Rovers board and he signed for the Toffees on 10 March, after temporarily leaving the England squad that he had been called up for.

Other potential suitors had included Leeds – who submitted a £120,000 bid for Fred and Mike England but were turned down – Wolves, Sunderland and Tottenham. The fee was £85,000 – a record between two English clubs at the time. Pickering had scored 59 league goals in 123 games for his home-town club.

The lifting of the maximum wage in 1961 had worked against Blackburn as the Rovers board were unable to match his wage demands. Fred later quoted that he moved to Everton to compete for trophies, earn higher wages and to play in Europe – nothing much changes in football, whatever the era!

Fred made his Everton debut on Saturday 11 March versus Nottingham Forest, replacing Alex Young in the line-up, a decision that was not universally popular with the Goodison faithful. However, he opened his Everton account on seven minutes with a crisp volley, scored again with a long-range shot, before completing his hat-trick before half-time.

Left: Fred Pickering being congratulated by Everton captain Roy Vernon on scoring a hat-trick on his debut.
Right: a cartoon style report – synonymous of the times – of Fred's hat-trick.

Everton won the game 6-1, with Fred starring and immediately feted by Everton fans as a future legend. He also achieved the unusual feat of scoring a hat-trick for and against Everton at Goodison Park in the same season. Fred ended the season with nine goals in nine appearances.

Fred was outstanding in the 1964/65 season, scoring 37 goals in all competitions, and was at his peak as an Everton footballer, endearing himself to Evertonians still further by scoring in a 4-0 win versus Liverpool.

He scored in seven successive fixtures and in eight consecutive home fixtures, but, despite this consistency, Everton could only manage fourth in the First Division that season, which was considered to be a disappointment in view of their investment and talent available.

Fred in typical goalscoring action for Everton against Burnley.

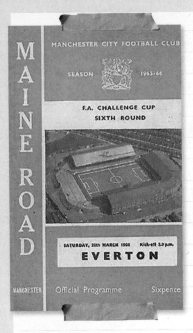

The following season (1965/66), Fred scored 22 times in all competitions, including some valuable FA Cup goals. However, tragedy struck during a 0-0 draw versus Liverpool in March, when he was carried off after collapsing under no pressure with a problem with his right knee.

As a result, he missed the FA Cup quarter-final tie (plus the first replay) versus Manchester City, but returned for the second replay at Molineux, scoring a fantastic volley in a 2-0 victory for Everton.

The programme for the FA Cup quarter-final tie versus Manchester City.

Another injury meant that he missed the semi-final versus Manchester United, which Everton won 1-0 thanks to a Colin Harvey goal. Although Fred did play in the next four league fixtures, he was told the day before the FA Cup Final versus Sheffield Wednesday that he wasn't selected as manager Catterick did not believe that he was fit enough.

This was a serious blow to Fred, and his relationship with Catterick never recovered. Fred maintained, in the strongest possible terms, his fitness for the final and carried that sense of injustice to his dying days.

Fred, in his overcoat, enjoying a drink with Colin Harvey – front centre – who scored the goal to take Everton to Wembley in 1966.

Pickering's replacement – Mike Trebilcock – scored twice as Everton came back from 2-0 down to win 3-2. However, Fred didn't attend the winners' banquet held by the Lord Mayor in Liverpool. Pickering was clearly very hurt by missing out on the biggest game of his career and submitted a transfer request in July 1966, which was rejected by the Everton board.

However, the 1966/67 season was Pickering's last as an Everton player as injuries continued to hamper his progress, including a cartilage operation. His two goals versus Aston Villa in May 1967, in a 4-2 win at Villa Park, were his last for the Toffees and he left in the summer of 1967, still only 26 years old, and with a record in all competitions of 70 goals in 115 Everton appearances.

Following his Goodison departure, Pickering surprisingly signed for second division Birmingham City in August 1967 for £50,000, spending two seasons in the West Midlands, becoming a fans' favourite once again with his barn-storming style. The season was memorable for the FA Cup run that took the Blues to the semi-final, with Fred scoring a majestic header to beat Chelsea in the sixth round. Sadly for Fred, Birmingham were beaten 2-0 by eventual winners West Brom, despite Pickering playing his heart out, striking the frame of the goal twice – the football gods clearly deciding that a cup final was just not to be for Fred Pickering!

Fred Pickering scoring for Birmingham City v Chelsea in the sixth round of the 1967/68 FA Cup – a famous goal in Birmingham City's history.

That run, however, cost them promotion and Fred returned to Lancashire, signing for Blackpool. Once again he endeared himself with the fans by scoring a hat-trick in a 3-0 win versus local rivals Preston North End in 1970 – a win that promoted the Seasiders back to the First Division and effectively relegated North End!

Fred Pickering at Birmingham City.

Fred returned to Blackburn in March 1971, with Rovers fighting relegation to Division Three. Sadly he was unable to save them, as injuries and being 'overweight' (quoted from *Blackburn Rovers Official History*) meant that he was a shadow of the player who left seven years previously. He was released in February 1972 and after a fruitless two-month trial at Brighton he retired and found work as a forklift driver in Blackburn.

At his peak, he was capped three times for England in 1964, bagging five goals, including a hat-trick versus the USA on his international debut at Randall's Island, New York, which England won 10-0. Fred was in Alf Ramsey's provisional squad of 40 for the 1966 World Cup, but his injuries not only cost him a place in the FA Cup Final but also in the final World Cup 22, and in that respect he can be considered an unlucky footballer at a key time in his career.

Fred was a regular scorer throughout his career, earning him the nickname 'Boomer' because of his strong shot, and he ended his career with a healthy tally of 168 goals in 354 league goals, albeit not all in the top flight.

Fred Pickering passed away in February 2019, aged 78, and leaves many fond memories at all of his clubs. They don't make them like 'Boomer' anymore. Rest In Peace.

PLAYER PROFILE
Matthew Andrew McEvoy

Born on 15 July 1938 in Dublin, Andy McEvoy is exactly the sort of player that this book is about – joint-top and second-top goalscorer in the First Division for two seasons and yet he remains largely unknown, partly due to his modesty and humility.

He was playing for his local Irish Republic side Bray Wanderers when he was spotted by the legendary Jackie Carey and recommended to Blackburn, who signed him in October 1956.

Despite scoring twice on his Blackburn debut, playing as an inside-forward versus Luton Town in April 1959, he was soon switched to wing-half. However, he was in-and-out of the team

McEvoy in Blackburn colours.

for a couple of seasons before being converted back to a forward by manager 'Jolly' Jack Marshall. He played up front with Fred Pickering in the third game of the 1963/64 season, despite not even being selected for the opening fixture that season, at home to eventual champions Liverpool, which Blackburn lost 2-1.

This impressive Blackburn Rovers team were nicknamed 'Marshall's Misfits' owing to cash-strapped manager Jack Marshall having to compensate for being unable to sign new players by converting existing squad players into new positions – e.g. Mike England was converted from full-back to centre-half (later with distinction for both Spurs and Wales), and Bryan Douglas moved from right-wing to inside-forward with ease, scoring 100 times from 400 appearances in his new position.

Both Pickering and McEvoy were switched from half- and full-backs into forwards to form a devastating strike partnership – one of the best in the league at that time.

The switch up-front worked wonders immediately, with a goal in the third game of the season, a 2-1 away win at Villa Park, and exploded into life with four goals in a 7-2 mauling of Tottenham Hotspur on 7 September.

Thereafter, McEvoy was a regular scorer as he developed a lethal partnership with Fred Pickering: two at Leicester in October, three in a 3-1 win at Wolves in November, followed a week later by a goal in the 4-1 home win versus Arsenal, with Pickering netting a hat-trick.

By now the London-based national press were beginning to take note, as Blackburn headed to the top of the table after a superb 2-1 win at Liverpool on 14 December, with two more from Andy McEvoy.
That win set Blackburn up nicely for the Upton Park mauling that kept Rovers at the summit, despite losing the return fixture a week later.

Although Rovers faded badly in the spring of 1963/64, McEvoy was the second top scorer in the First Division with 32 goals, just three behind a certain Jimmy Greaves.

McEvoy scoring at Anfield.

The following season he scored 29 goals, despite losing his strike partner, Pickering, to Everton in March the previous season, and despite Blackburn finishing the season in tenth position. His goal tally that season earned him the joint-top First Division goalscorer honour with Greaves.

This was a significant achievement for the modest Irishman, who put his success down to being 'in the right place at the right time', which we all know is a rare talent, especially in crowded penalty areas, which is where McEvoy plundered most of his goals. He was a real predator, who developed a poacher's instinct similar to that of the deadly Greaves and Roger Hunt.

His team-mates respected his ability, and are on record as saying that McEvoy was 'two-footed, well balanced, a clinical taker of chances, often appearing to pass the ball into the net wide of the keeper, and with absolutely no trace of an ego'. McEvoy himself was embarrassed by this adulation and fame did not sit easy with him.

In season 1965/66, Blackburn were relegated, knocking the stuffing out of McEvoy, and although he played one more season (in Division Two in 1966/67), his motivation had gone. He informed the club that he wanted to return home to Ireland – he had suffered from homesickness many times during his career and his love for his homeland proved too strong this time.

Rovers graciously accepted his request and in 1967 they sold McEvoy for a modest fee to Limerick FC on the condition that if he ever returned to English football he would re-sign for Blackburn.

Both parties knew, however, that the prospect of this happening was zero, even though McEvoy was just 29 years old and at his peak as a footballer. Fans and players alike thought that McEvoy had left England prematurely.

McEvoy had an eventful career with his national side, the Republic of Ireland, and when selected to play his routine was always the same; visit his family in Bray (just south of Dublin), including his father Lally, who was also an accomplished footballer, then call into his local hostelry for a couple of pints and scrambled eggs on toast!

He often carried his boots in a carrier bag and it was this laid back attitude that some felt did not always endear him to his national team-mates. Some established members of the squad could not relate to McEvoy's belief that football was not the 'be all and end all' of life, believing that McEvoy never truly utilised his skills and natural talent.

THE IRISH PRESS, MONDAY, OCTOBER 26, 1964

McEVOY THE MAGNIFICENT !

SATURDAY—TWO FOR HIS CLUB... crashes home a goal in each half to help Blackburn come from behind to beat Everton 3-2.

☆ ☆ ☆ ☆ ☆

☆ ☆ ☆ ☆ ☆

SUNDAY—TWO FOR HIS COUNTRY ... one in each half again and he races away after scoring the second which helped Ireland come from behind to beat Poland 3-2.

A situation typical of the era: McEvoy played for Blackburn versus Everton at Goodison Park on 24 October 1964, scoring twice as Rovers came from behind to win 3-2 ... and then, the very next day, scored another two, as the Republic came from 2-0 down to beat Poland 3-2 in front of 42,000 in Dublin. Two 'come-back' wins in two days for two teams in two countries. Modern strength and conditioning coaches would not be happy!

republic of
IRELAND
v
SPAIN
Wed 8 April 1964

DALYMOUNT PARK

EUROPEAN NATIONS CUP

OFFICAL programme 6d

The programme for the second leg of the 1964 European Championship quarter-final between the Republic of Ireland and Spain.

Spain won both legs – 5-1 in Seville (McEvoy scored the Irish goal) and 2-0 in Dublin – to secure a comprehensive 7-1 aggregate victory.

He scord six times in 17 appearances, including a brace against Poland in Dublin in 1964. McEvoy also played in the qualifying games for the 1966 World Cup, and football historians often overlook the fact that the Republic of Ireland came very close to qualifying for the finals, which were, of course, held across the Irish Sea in England.

It was an era of four countries per qualifying group, but bizarrely the Republic were drawn in a group of just three – Group 9 – which included Spain and Syria. Even more bizarrely, Syria withdrew from the competition, in solidarity with African countries, who had boycotted the tournament in protest against FIFA's miserly finals allocation for Africa of just one place.

Thus, Group 9 consisted of just two countries. Incidentally, it was this boycotting that enabled North Korea to qualify for the 1966 World Cup. McEvoy played in the first leg at Dalymount Park, Dublin, which the Irish won 1-0 courtesy of an own goal from Spaniard Jose Angel Iribar.

In the return leg in Seville, in October 1965, five months after the home leg, Andy McEvoy gave the Irish hope with a goal after 26 minutes, but four unanswered goals from the Spaniards secured a home win. However, the rules of the competition dictated that the tie finished one win each (no aggregate scores applied), resulting in a play-off to decide who competed in the finals in England.

The fixture, on 10 November 1965, became one of the most controversial games in Irish football history and began a long list of qualifying agonies for the Irish.

The tie was originally scheduled to be played at neutral Highbury, in North London – the preferred venue for FIFA and an ideal venue for the large Irish population in that area, guaranteeing a large, vocal 'home' support for the Republic. However, the FAI then entered into what are politely called 'negotiations' with the Spanish FA, with the outcome being that the fixture was switched to Paris, after the Spanish agreed to give up their share of the gate receipts, thus securing the Irish £25,000 – three times their income from the previous year.

Not surprisingly, there was almost no Irish support in Paris and, despite a real fight, they lost 1-0 to a goal 11 minutes from time.

Eamonn Dunphy – later to become a distinguished writer and broadcaster – made his debut that day and was scathing about the conduct of the FAI, who traded short-term funding for a chance to reach the World Cup finals … and secure income that would have dwarfed that £25,000. Andy McEvoy and the rest of that Republic of Ireland squad would never again come close to qualifying for a major tournament.

After leaving Blackburn Rovers and ending his international career in 1967, McEvoy played for part-time Limerick in the Irish League, who trained twice a week, with players holding down other jobs.

Whilst there, he built up an impressive portfolio of goals, including a majestic 25-yard volley at Waterford.

In truth he was too good for that level, but he was happy and that mattered to him above all else. He enjoyed a wonderfully happy five years there, winning the Irish cup and combined playing with a steady job as a driver for Guinness. It is reported that he sometimes missed training due to work commitments, but his manager and team-mates were not bothered as his presence often helped the team secure win bonuses and trophies in big games.

An indication of his modesty came in the early 1990s when Blackburn Rovers were featured on satellite TV in a bar where he was having a drink, and Alan Shearer was quoted as being the league's leading scorer. The host returned a question as to the last time a Blackburn Rovers player was the top goalscorer in the top flight.

40 years on and Limerick celebrate historic first FAI Cup

Standing: Jack Tuohy (secretary), Willie Flaherty, Hughie Hamilton, Ritchie Hall, Kevin Fitzpatrick, Joe O'Mahony, Tony Meaney, Seam? Coad, Michael Wallace (chairman) , Ewan Fenton (manager)
...nt: Billy Higgins (director) Sean Byrnes, Joe Bourke, Al Finucane (captain), Paddy Shortt, Andy McEvoy, and Dave Barrett.

The Limerick team that lifted the FAI Cup for the first time in their history in season 1970/71.

Knowing that he was the answer, Andy McEvoy went to hide in the lavatory to avoid being in the room when the question was answered. He was a very humble man but did accept an offer for one of the local leagues in the Republic of Ireland to be named after him.

After ending his playing days, Andy lived happily in Bray, working at the ICI warehouse, whilst helping his local team Bray Wanderers, who eventually joined the League of Ireland in 1985. He also helped out with his old junior club Glenview on a few occasions.

He lived with his wife Phil, whom he had met in England, but who hailed from County Clare. They had four children – two of whom were handy players themselves (Brian and Andy Junior).

Andy sadly passed away in May 1994, aged just 55, after a short illness.

———

Andy McEvoy scored 61 First Division goals in two magical seasons, mixing it with legends of the game for that period – Roger Hunt, Jimmy Greaves, Denis Law, to name but a few.

He was super talented but he would consider it more important that we note he was a family man, honest and quiet, humble and under-stated.

Rest In Peace Andy. Fans in East Lancashire will never forget your contribution to that exceptional Blackburn Rovers side.

PLAYER PROFILE
John Joseph Byrne

Born in West Horsley, Surrey, on 13 May 1939, at the outset of World War Two, Johnny Byrne was universally known in the football world as 'Budgie' Byrne due to his incessant chatter. Although not technically a Cockney by birth, he displayed all the attributes of one: bright, chatty, outspoken, sociable, cheeky and streetwise. But, make no mistake, Byrne was an outstanding and gifted footballer – one of the best of his era.

He showed early promise in youth football in Epsom and Guildford, before signing as a professional with Crystal Palace in 1956 on his 17th birthday after being recommended by his ex-schoolteacher Vincent Blore (an ex-professional with Palace and West Ham). Johnny was working as an apprentice toolmaker at the time, having left school at 15.

He had an excellent five-year career with Crystal Palace, achieving promotion to Division Three in 1960/61, and is fondly remembered by Palace fans from that era. During his Palace career, he achieved the rare feat of playing for England Under 23s as a fourth-tier player and, incredibly, played a full 90 minutes for England (versus Northern Ireland in November 1961 at Wembley) as a third-tier player.

England drew that fixture 1-1 in the Home Championships with a goal from Bobby Charlton, and Byrne did not look out of place in an England shirt. By the time he was transferred to Division One side West Ham, Byrne had scored 85 goals in 203 appearances for Crystal Palace, but all in the bottom two tiers of English football. However, his talent was there for all to see.

Left: 'Budgie' Byrne at Crystal Palace.
Right: In action at West Ham.

His transfer was inevitable given his success at Palace, along with his England call-up, and he signed for a then substantial fee of £65,000, which included West Ham reserve Ron Brett (valued at £7,000) going in the opposite direction. Sadly Ron was killed in August 1962, aged just 24, when his car hit a lorry in Camberwell, after only 13 appearances for Palace.

Originally, West Ham manager Ron Greenwood was open to the idea of Geoff Hurst being part of the deal instead of Brett, but changed his mind as he wanted Hurst to play up-front, with Byrne just off him – a plan designed to allow Byrne's talent to shine, whilst Hurst did all the hard running. The life of Geoff Hurst could have been oh-so-different, had Greenwood stuck to his initial plan.

Interestingly, West Ham were unable to pay the full cash element of the transfer fee (£58,000), instead agreeing with Palace to pay £1,000 per week, until it was paid off – a sort of 'hire-purchase' transfer. Byrne's initial salary with the Hammers was £40 per week – approximately double the wage of the average skilled worker at that time.

Byrne settled in at West Ham and, after a slow start adjusting to the style of play that manager Greenwood wanted, became a Hammers legend, winning the prestigious 'Hammer of the Year' in 1963/64. He was outstanding as the Hammers went on an FA Cup run, scoring in four rounds. The Hammers beat Charlton Athletic, Leyton Orient (after a replay), Swindon, Burnley, Manchester United in the semi-final (winning 3-1), before beating Preston in the final.

Likened to the legend Alfredo di Stefano in playing style, Byrne was a stocky man, only 5ft 8in but a solid 12 stone, although, you could argue, with slightly bandy legs. However, he was a gifted, intelligent footballer, adept at finding space by 'dropping off' the centre-half and bringing others into play. He was particularly good at playing with his back to goal, as well as being a prolific taker of chances.

Johnny would have been a strong candidate to represent his country at the 1962 World Cup in Chile, but was shunned by the selectors after a confrontation in the tunnel at The Hawthorns with West Bromwich Albion's Don Howe, which the FA disapproved of. However, he returned to the England fold and in total won 11 caps, scoring eight goals for his country, which could, and should, have been many more.

Highlights of his international career included scoring a brace, as England beat Switzerland 8-1 and a memorable hat-trick in a pulsating 4-3 win in Lisbon on 17 May 1964, against a Portugal team that included Eusebio. Bobby Charlton also scored for England that

Johnny Byrne with his good friend Bobby Moore, pictured before the fixture versus Scotland in April 1965 at Wembley, a game that would change his career.

evening and five of that starting XI went on to play in the World Cup Final at Wembley, some 26 months later. However, Byrne missed out on the 1966 World Cup squad in tragic circumstances.

Byrne started for England versus the Scots, at Wembley in April 1965, just 12 months or so before the World Cup finals began. England – with nine of the 11 who went on to play in the World Cup Final – quickly went 2-0 up, with goals from Bobby Charlton and Jimmy Greaves. But then they lost left-back Ray Wilson to an injury and, with no substitutions, Johnny Byrne filled in, as England went down to ten men. Then Byrne himself got injured, badly damaging knee ligaments, but played on, thus compounding the injury. The game ended 2-2, with Denis Law and Ian St John scoring for Scotland.

The injury forced Byrne to miss West Ham's European Cup Winners' Cup Final v 1860 Munich, and there is an argument to suggest that he wasn't quite the same player thereafter. By the time he was fit, Alf Ramsey had enough cover in his England squad and Byrne missed out on selection for the tournament. The Scotland game was his last in an England shirt.

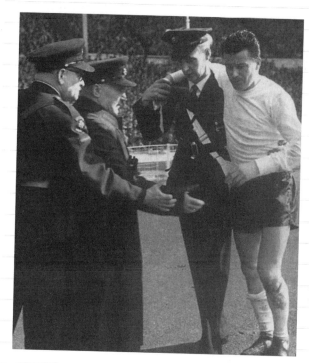

Johnny being helped off at Wembley in 1965 by St. John's medical staff, with England's medical team nowhere in sight!

By 1967 Byrne had regained his fitness fully, but it was felt that, at just 28 years old, he was already past his best, and he left West Ham to return to Crystal Palace. He had enjoyed a highly successful career at Upton Park, scoring 108 goals in 206 games in all competitions.

For at least two seasons (1963-1965, when he scored 60 goals in 90 games) he was considered to be amongst the best in the First Division, and is rightly regarded as a Hammers legend.

Byrne could be portrayed as a 'wind-up merchant', and an incident involving West Ham's physio Bill Jenkins confirms this. Byrne wound Bill up so much that he lunged at Budgie, only for Byrne to sway out of the way, causing Bill's face to crash into scaffolding, resulting in a badly gashed head. Jenkins was a tough East Ender and asked to be taken home to be stitched up by his wife, rather than go to A&E. As he left, he advised Byrne that 'it might be a good idea if you don't get injured for a while.'

Byrne re-signed for Palace in February 1967 for a fee of £45,000, considered to be great business by West Ham. The Palace chairman Arthur Wait signed Byrne with half-an-eye on the commercial side, believing Byrne's popularity would drive higher gates. However, there were two problems that caused manager Bert Head and Arthur to clash regularly over the next year or so:

(1) Byrne was, by now, thicker around the middle and the quick bursts had gone.

(2) Arthur Wait did not consult the manager Bert, who was not onside with the transfer, as he had no desire to have an opinionated, flamboyant and over-the-hill footballer at his club.

Byrne did not have a successful time in his second spell for Palace, playing only 36 games in Division Two, scoring just five goals, and fans started to turn on him. His weight issues were also a concern, even for Alf Ramsey, who nicknamed him 'Toby Jug' but still selected him for an FA tour to Canada in 1967, as he was good for team morale.

The working relationship between Head and Byrne deteriorated, and when the Palace management met their Fulham counterparts at Manchester station (both on their way home, after away games in the latter part of the 1967/68 season), Fulham manager Bobby Robson signed Johnny for £25,000 on the train, with 15 minutes to go before the deadline.

However, Byrne couldn't save them from relegation and his spell at Craven Cottage was equally unsuccessful. He scored three goals in 19 games, some of which were as a central defender. He played his final game in England for Fulham, ironically at Selhurst Park, in April 1969, shortly before his 30th birthday.

Byrne then spent four years playing in South Africa, for the now defunct Durban City, before taking on a variety of coaching and managerial roles in the same continent for 30 years. He died from a heart attack in Cape Town in 1999, aged just 60.

He left behind a legacy of outstanding goals and, on his day (and there were plenty of those), he was amongst the best footballers of his generation.

Thanks for the memories Johnny, and Rest In Peace.

Johnny Byrne during his time in South Africa, where he made a significant contribution to football.

BLACKPOOL

BLACKPOOL
FOOTBALL CLUB

OFFICIAL PROGRAMME
4d.

THURSDAY, 26th DECEMBER, 1963
KICK-OFF 2.0 p.m.

CHELSEA

Chapter 3

Blackpool v Chelsea

1 - 5

Kick-off: 3pm   Venue: Bloomfield Road   Attendance: 17,563

Waiters	1	Bonetti
Thompson	2	Hinton
Martin	3	McCreadie
McPhee	4	Harris
Gratix	5	Mortimore
Cranston	6	Upton
Hill	7	Murray ⚽
⚽ Durie	8	Houseman ⚽
Charnley	9	Bridges ⚽⚽
Parry	10	Venables ⚽
Horne	11	Blunstone

The Managers

Ron Suart   Tommy Docherty

Match Report

We begin the afternoon kick-offs in the famous north-west town of Blackpool, with its grand old club 'The Seasiders', who were a regular First Division outfit in the early 60s. They had also been regular visitors to Wembley for the FA Cup Final – in 1948 (lost), 1951 (lost) and in 1953, in possibly the most memorable FA Cup Final of them all, when Blackpool beat Bolton Wanderers 4-3, in what later became known as the 'Matthews Final', even though it was Stan Mortensen who scored the hat-trick for Blackpool.

In the decade since winning the cup, Blackpool finished in the top half of the First Division on several occasions and their squad for season 1963/64 still contained some quality players. However, it was becoming a struggle to stay in the top flight; a situation made harder when the maximum wage regulation was lifted, the impact of which began to bite in the next decade.

Blackpool, managed by Ron Suart, had a couple of influential injuries to contend with, being without full-back Jimmy Armfield and the burgeoning talent of Alan Ball.

Blackpool stars, Alan Ball (left) and Jimmy Armfield (right).

Chelsea in 1963'64.

Chelsea, under Tommy Docherty, had been promoted just 18 months previously and were a developing team, full of energy and young players from their youth programme, many of whom would go on to become Chelsea legends, tasting success several years later, winning the FA Cup in 1969/70 and the European Cup Winners' Cup 12 months later.

The Chelsea line-up for their Boxing Day fixture included Blues legends Ron 'Chopper' Harris, future Chelsea manager Eddie McCreadie, future England goalkeeper Peter Bonetti and future England manager Terry Venables. The squad travelled north on Christmas Eve, spending Christmas Day in a Blackpool hotel, the Norbeck Castle, whilst training on Blackpool beach during the day.

Wearing their famous tangerine colours, Blackpool kicked off on a cold afternoon on the coast, but it was Chelsea, in their famous blue, who were immediately in the ascendancy, with Barry Bridges putting them ahead after just two minutes, reacting quickest to a loose ball. Chelsea continued to dominate and Albert Murray put the Blues further ahead after 20 minutes with a sharp finish, and Blackpool had it all to do. The Seasiders pushed forward in an attempt to get a foothold in the game and, as half-time approached, they were unlucky when a couple of attempts at goal flashed wide.

However, Chelsea were playing with a style that manager Docherty had instilled in them – high-energy football with quick, sharp passing, along with innovative tactics, such as over-lapping full-backs.

Blackpool in 1963/64.

Sadly for Blackpool, Chelsea took the fixture away from them with two goals just before half-time. The first came from 18-year-old winger Peter Houseman (his first goal in a distinguished Chelsea career) from just outside the box. The second was another typical Bridges goal, on the stroke of the half-time whistle, when he caught Blackpool on the break with his speed to slide in Chelsea's fourth.

Game over you would think, as the teams headed down the tunnel with Chelsea leading 4-0. The *Daily Mirror* concurred, and their report of the day indicated that 'everyone could have gone home by half-time', such was Chelsea's dominance and clinical finishing.

Blackpool made some tactical tweaks during the break and, as a result, were tighter defensively in the second half. They managed to pull one goal back on 63 minutes, through a powerful shot from inside-forward Dave Durie, to give them a glimmer of hope. However, Terry Venables scored from outside the box just three minutes later to quell any Blackpool revival. Chelsea saw out the remaining 24 minutes of the game with ease, winning 5-1.

The impressive away-day victory took the Blues to seventh in the table, but Blackpool had an immediate chance for revenge as both teams travelled south to meet again, just 48 hours later in West London.

Return Match

**Chelsea
1-0
Blackpool**

Date: 28 December   **Venue:** Stamford Bridge   **Att:** 34,380

Blackpool travelled south to London hoping for better fortunes than their previous trips to the capital earlier that season had yielded; they had shipped six at Spurs (lost 1-6), five at Arsenal (lost 3-5) and three at West Ham (lost 1-3)!

Chelsea's win at Bloomfield Road had lifted them to seventh in the table, and for the return fixture in West London neither side made any team changes, which meant that Blackpool were still without Jimmy Armfield and a young Alan Ball, who was a big player for Blackpool that season – he ended up top league goalscorer with 13 goals from the inside-right position, a great effort for an 18-year-old.

The game kicked off and another early goal from Barry Bridges, using his predatory instincts and lightning speed, put the Blues ahead inside five minutes, for the second consecutive fixture. After going behind early on, Blackpool were once again without much of a cutting edge, although they did force Chelsea keeper Bonetti to make two outstanding saves, to prevent the Seasiders from equalising.

Bonetti's saves were not only superb but courageous too, as it was later revealed that he had broken a finger during the game. As a consequence, Bonetti missed the next fixture, replaced by his deputy John Dunn.

Despite some Blackpool pressure, Chelsea saw out the fixture relatively comfortably, winning 1-0, enabling them to save some energy for their big FA Cup third-round fixture the following week, when they played Spurs at White Hart Lane. They drew that game 1-1, but won the replay 2-0, despite the absence of Bonetti.

In truth, the return fixture was a largely drab affair, with the 34,380 present at Stamford Bridge that day hoping for a little more holiday entertainment. However, the victory kept this emerging, young vibrant Chelsea team in the top six.

By the end of the season, Chelsea had improved slightly to finish fifth, representing a great effort for a promoted club. Blackpool, however, struggled to score goals all season but survived, just, by finishing 18th.

The two clubs then went in separate directions in the following years, with Chelsea playing in the 1967 and 1970 FA Cup finals, famously winning the latter in a replay versus Leeds United at Old Trafford. With some Chelsea legends in their midst, they went on to land the European Cup Winners' Cup the following season, beating Real Madrid in Athens after a replay.

Blackpool continued to decline after the early 60s, with their days as a regular top-flight club and competing for trophies sadly coming to an end. They sold Alan Ball after the 1966 World Cup to Everton for £112,000 and that, along with other sales such as Emlyn Hughes, precipitated a further decline in their fortunes. They were eventually relegated in season 1966/67, finishing bottom with only six wins, and despite being promoted in 1969/70 (the crucial fixture being a 3-0 win at Preston in front of 34,000, with 20,000 Blackpool fans present) they finished bottom once again in 1970/71, with just four wins.

The lifting of the maximum wage hit clubs like Blackpool hard and they settled down to become a competitive Division Two club in the 70s, before being relegated to Division Three in 1977/78. Their slide continued as they dropped into Division Four in 1981 – a sad decline indeed for a famous club with such a rich heritage and history. They did, however, reach the Premier League in season 2010/11, under Ian Holloway. But their stay was short lived as they finished in 19th position and were relegated back to the Championship. It is hoped that, under new ownership, they can once again challenge to win that place back.

PLAYER PROFILE
Barry John Bridges

Born in Horsford, Norfolk, on 29 April 1941, Bridges was a fusion of rapid pace and a natural goalscoring instinct, making him very difficult to defend against.

He was a schoolboy sprint champion, which served him well when he became a professional footballer. He played for Norfolk Schools, represented England Schoolboys and, not surprisingly, attracted interest from Norwich City. However, they were in Division Three at the time and the young Bridges wanted to test himself at the highest level. After being invited for a trial, he signed for Chelsea, whereupon he met Bobby Tambling, who would become a life-long friend after living together in digs for five years.

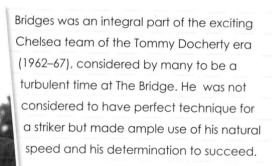

Bridges was an integral part of the exciting Chelsea team of the Tommy Docherty era (1962–67), considered by many to be a turbulent time at The Bridge. He was not considered to have perfect technique for a striker but made ample use of his natural speed and his determination to succeed.

Bridges made a good impression in the Chelsea youth ranks and made his first-team debut, aged just 17 in February 1959, scoring in a 3-2 win versus West Ham United. However, a couple of seasons passed until he could be considered a regular and that was in a Chelsea side destined for relegation in 1961/62. Despite the poor team, Bridges scored an impressive 19 goals in 32 appearances.

Down in the second tier, however, Bridges did not enjoy such success and was eventually dropped for Frank Upton, late in the season, as Chelsea secured promotion and a swift return to the top flight. Although back in the big time, Bridges was not selected initially but wouldn't have to wait too long to reform his lethal partnership with one of Chelsea's all-time greats, Bobby Tambling.

Bridges was so quick that many of his goals were garnered from being first to pounce on loose balls in the box. His other preferred method of scoring was to play on the shoulder of the last defender, before running on to through balls 'in the channel', often played by Venables, who was a fine passer of a football. It was a tactic that worked often for Chelsea, although Bridges was perhaps caught offside more than he should have been.

Sadly for Bridges, his Chelsea career never really recovered from his involvement in what became known as 'The Chelsea Eight' (where eight players broke a curfew and were sent home as a result). The Blues were due to play their last three fixtures of season 1964/65 away in the North West and chose to stay at the Norbeck Castle Hotel in Blackpool for the duration, rather than travel back and forth to London. They were still in with a chance of winning the title before these games commenced, but lost the first 2-0 to Liverpool on Easter Monday. With five days until their next game, the players became bored, and so eight of them broke the curfew, leaving through a fire exit to enjoy Blackpool's nightlife.

However, the group had not reckoned on a sharp-eyed hotel employee, who alerted manager Docherty to the fire-exit door being ajar. Docherty decided to set up a vigil (allegedly in a fluffy white dressing gown), until the players rolled in … which they did at 4am, somewhat worse for wear. All eight players – first teamers Bridges, Hollins, Graham, McCreadie, Murray, Hinton, and Venables, along with reserve-team player Joe Fascione, were sent home in disgrace – a tough call by Docherty with the league title still on the line.

With a much weakened team, Chelsea duly lost their next game 6-2 at Burnley on the Saturday, with the side including two players for whom this was their one-and-only Chelsea appearance. Burnley's Andy Lochhead, whom we will meet in the next chapter, scored five against a makeshift Chelsea defence.

The disgraced players were recalled for the final fixture at Blackpool on the Monday – a game they also lost – to conclude a bizarre end to the season for Chelsea. Within 12 months, five of the 'Chelsea eight' had left the club, including Bridges, as his working relationship with the autocratic Scotsman Docherty never fully recovered. The end was nigh for Bridges when he was dropped in a fixture versus Leicester in October 1965, for the developing, prodigious talent of Peter Osgood, who had been promised a run of 12 fixtures in the side. Bridges was a little miffed, as, pre-World Cup, he wanted to play to impress Alf Ramsey. Chelsea fans were angry too, raising a petition in protest that he may be allowed to leave.

Bridges did win his place back for the FA Cup fifth-round tie versus Shrewsbury. Playing wide, he scored twice, including a swerving right-foot drive confirming his contribution in a 3-2 victory. However, he was once again dropped after the semi-final defeat to Sheffield Wednesday and was overlooked for the Inter Cities Fairs Cup fixture in Barcelona in 1966, being sent home from the airport. As a result, Bridges's departure was inevitable.

Bridges scoring for Chelsea in 1965 versus Fulham at Craven Cottage.

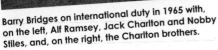
Barry Bridges on international duty in 1965 with, on the left, Alf Ramsey, Jack Charlton and Nobby Stiles, and, on the right, the Charlton brothers.

Whilst at Chelsea, Bridges scored 93 goals in 203 appearances, winning the League Cup once in 1964/65 (beating Leicester City over two legs), and remains a fans' favourite to this day. He gained four England caps – his first versus Scotland at Wembley in April 1965 – followed by further caps against Hungary and Yugoslavia in Belgrade, where Bridges scored his only England goal. His final cap was in October 1965 versus Austria, but after losing his Chelsea place and getting injured he was not selected again.

Somewhat surprisingly for an international footballer and still only 25, Bridges signed for Birmingham City, then in the division below, for £55,000 - a club record.

No doubt Bridges would have taken great pleasure when Birmingham surprisingly beat Chelsea 1-0 in the FA Cup sixth round in 1967/68. He scored regularly at St Andrew's over two and a half seasons, scoring 37 times in 83 appearances before returning to the capital, playing for two seasons at Queens Park Rangers (32 goals in 72 fixtures), two seasons at Millwall (27 goals in 77 fixtures) and finally for two seasons at Brighton (14 goals in 66 fixtures).

Barry Bridges at QPR.

One legacy of Bridges's time at Chelsea is that he met his Polish wife Irena whilst at the club, and her father kept a café on the Fulham Road, where players would meet regularly for a quality breakfast.

Bridges was instinctive, pacy and incisive, and he scored goals wherever he played. His career record of 189 senior goals in 474 appearances demonstrates a significant talent over a 16-year career.

After his playing days were over, Barry moved to Ireland as player-manager of St Patricks and then Sligo Rovers, before returning to England to manage Dereham Town, King's Lynn and Horsford FC. He then ran his family farm and a newsagency. As at 2019, Barry is 78 years old, in robust health and living in Norfolk. He is often a guest at Stamford Bridge and always receives a great reception from the Chelsea faithful.

Bravo Sir on a great career.

BURNLEY

FOOTBALL CLUB

SEASON 1963-64

F.A. Cup Winners 1913-14   F.A. Cup Finalists 1946-47, 1961-62
League Champions Div. I 1920-21, 1959-60. Runners-up 1919-20, 1961-63
League Champions Div. II 1897-98   Runners-up 1912-13, 1946-47
League Champions Central League 1902-03, 1961-62, 1962-63
Lancashire Senior Cup Winners 1889, 1915, 1958, 1952, 1960, 1961, 1962
Record number of 30 consecutive 1st Division League games
without defeat 1920-21

No. 13 Manchester Utd   26th December, 1963

OFFICIAL PROGRAMME   4ᴰ

Published by The Burnley Football and Athletic Co. Ltd.

Chapter 4

Burnley v Manchester United

6 - 1

Kick-off: 3pm   **Venue: Turf Moor**   **Attendance: 35,754**

Burnley		Manchester United
Blacklaw	1	Gaskell
Angus	2	Dunne
Elder	3	Cantwell
O'Neil	4	Crerand
Talbot	5	Foulkes
Miller	6	Setters
⚽⚽ Morgan	7	Quixall
Pointer	8	Moore
⚽⚽⚽⚽ Lochhead	9	Charlton
Harris	10	Herd ⚽
Towers	11	Brennan

The Managers
Harry Potts   Matt Busby

Match Report

After ten goals in East London and six on the coast at Blackpool, there was another incredible game at Turf Moor, as Burnley hit Manchester United for six, making 23 goals so far in the first three fixtures!

The scoreline at Turf Moor was perhaps not a major surprise, as Burnley were one of the top teams in the land at this point in time, achieving four successive top-four finishes, from 1959/60 to 1962/63, including a league-title win in 1959/60 – a wonderful feat for such a small town – and a runners-up spot in season 1961/62 (after winning just two of their final 13 fixtures). They also reached the FA Cup Final in the same season, losing 3-1 to Spurs. Their team was filled with some very talented footballers in that era, such as Jimmy McIlroy and Jimmy Adamson.

Burnley were a very progressive club at that time and were one of the first clubs to:

- invest in a purpose built training ground, whilst other clubs trained in schools and public parks

- develop a successful youth policy that garnered many quality footballers. The team that won the league only cost £13,000 in transfer fees – all the rest had developed through their youth scheme

- specialise and develop free-kick and set-piece routines, which were soon copied around the country.

Burnley in 1963/64.

Manchester United in 1963/64.

Like Blackpool, Burnley were ultimately hit hard by the abolition of the maximum wage, as relatively small provincial clubs could no longer compete financially with bigger city clubs. However, they did manage to maintain their status as a top-flight club throughout the 1960s, before being relegated in 1971.

Manchester United, meanwhile, had spent the previous five years recovering from the tragedy of the Munich air disaster in February 1958, when they sadly lost the majority of their 'Busby Babes' team. As a result, they only achieved a number of mid-table finishes during their rebuilding process but had shown a glimmer of promise by winning the FA Cup in 1962/63, despite finishing in the bottom four of the First Division. That league position was as bad as it got for United as they were on the cusp of some success in the league.

Going into the Boxing Day fixture, Burnley were ninth in the table and had already been involved in some high-scoring games that season, beating Everton 4-3, Fulham 4-1 and drawing 4-4 with Stoke City in November. The Red Devils, however, were competing at the top end of the table, sitting fourth on Christmas Day. They'd go on to finish second that season, beginning a successful spell of five years, culminating in winning the European Cup at Wembley in 1968.

Consistent with the era and the season, United had also featured in some high-scoring fixtures already, with 23 goals scored in their first four games, including victories against Everton (home, 5-1) and Ipswich Town (away, 7-2). However, in their previous fixture to this Boxing Day clash with Burnley, United had gone down 4-0 to Everton at Goodison Park, as the Toffees exacted their revenge for their heavy defeat at Old Trafford earlier in the season.

The game started at a cold Turf Moor on a greasy, difficult but playable pitch in front of 35,754 lucky souls (Burnley's highest gate of the season by 11,000), who would witness one of the most memorable victories in Burnley's history. It was a thrilling spectacle and kept up the tradition of previous Burnley/Manchester United fixtures from this era. United were completely over-run by 'sweet, slick and speedy Burnley forward play' (*Burnley Express*), with the win considered to be the best Burnley performance of the season, with Andy Lochhead and Willie Morgan owning the fixture.

Burnley took an early lead through Lochhead after just six minutes, following a fine move involving Angus, O'Neil and Morgan, who crossed for Pointer, to flick the ball onto Lochhead, who scored with a well-placed shot – 1-0.

David Herd levelled for United on 29 minutes, when he took advantage of some hesitancy in the home defence to latch onto a pass from Bobby Charlton to level the scoring – 1-1.

United, however, could not maintain parity, as a snap shot from Lochhead from distance deceived Gaskell in flight, giving Burnley a deserved lead three minutes before the break – 2-1 at half-time, and all to play for.

Lochhead's effort puts Burnley 1-0 up.

LOCHHEAD LEADS THE GOAL RUSH

By KEITH McNEE

How the local press reported Burnley's incredible victory.

The second half belonged to young Willie Morgan, who scored on 66 minutes after confusion in the United defence, following an O'Neil free kick – 3-1.

Burnley put the fixture to bed seven minutes later when Morgan turned provider with a pin-point cross for Lochhead, to score with a well-placed header for his hat-trick – 4-1.

With 17 minutes left, you might have expected both teams to settle down, but not a bit of it, as Paddy Crerand, United's combative right-half, was sent off after 77 minutes for striking Burnley's Towers right in front of referee Hussey, who had no hesitation in dismissing Crerand. Paddy, now a respected presenter on MUTV, was later to lament that he was unlucky to get his marching orders as, 'I only hit him once!'

Burnley utilised their extra man and extra space well, with Morgan scoring again with a brilliant left-foot shot into the corner – 5-1.

With United visibly tiring, Andy Lochhead scored his fourth and Burnley's sixth, with another fine shot in the last two minutes, to complete the scoring – 6-1.

Willie Morgan was to later tell the story of team-mate Andy Lochhead, who was devastated when he did not receive the match sponsor's 'Man-Of-The-Match' award, even though he'd scored four goals in the fixture. That accolade went to 18-year-old Morgan himself, who announced himself that day, with two goals and three assists in a memorable game. Some six years later, Morgan joined Manchester United, taking the iconic number 7 shirt, worn with distinction down the years by some outstanding footballers.

So, a fantastic win for Burnley, but the tables were turned just 48 hours later, when United, after two heavy away defeats in which they had conceded ten goals, got back on track – but how?

Return Match

Manchester United
5-1
Burnley

Date: 28 December   **Venue:** Old Trafford   **Att:** 47,834

Burnley travelled to Old Trafford trying to avoid a fourth successive away defeat, after losing at Spurs, Liverpool and Sheffield Wednesday. And they did so with a depleted team, after forwards Towers and Harris – who had both played well at Turf Moor – failed fitness tests.

United manager Matt Busby made some changes too, after the mauling at Turf Moor, by dropping wingers Quixall and Brennan, who had both been ineffective at Burnley. They were replaced by 16-year-old Willie Anderson – making his debut – and 17-year-old George Best, for only his second appearance for the club (he had made his debut that September versus West Bromwich Albion).

Best had actually gone home to Belfast for Christmas, with the club's blessing, believing that he would not be required for the holiday fixtures, but Busby sent a telegram to Best's family home requesting that he catch the first available flight back to Manchester, as he'd been selected to play.

Andy Lochhead continued his hot streak by scoring in the return fixture at Old Trafford. By then, however, Burnley were already five down, as the Red Devils completely turned the tables on the Clarets in a show of attacking power.

Burnley actually started the fixture well, with three decent chances in the first ten minutes. First of all, in the opening minute of the game, a Lochhead shot from distance nearly caught goalkeeper Gaskell off guard. Then Robson sent O'Neil through on goal unopposed, but Gaskell dived at his feet to prevent a certain goal. Finally, after eight minutes, Price shot wide after beating two United defenders. Three good attempts for the Clarets, but all spurned.

As so often happens in football, Burnley then went 1-0 down, as, against the run of play, United took the lead with their first meaningful attack. David Herd scored from a very narrow angle, following a bad back pass from Elder, who was destined not to enjoy his afternoon. Pointer hit the post for the Clarets but immediately afterwards Moore extended United's lead, as Burnley sensed that it was not going to be their day.

A memorable moment then arrived on 25 minutes when George Best scored the first goal of his legendary career from 20 yards after excellent build-up play involving Herd, Charlton and Anderson, although Elder could perhaps have defended better to prevent United increasing their lead. At 3-0 down, half-time could not come soon enough for Burnley.

A legendary moment in the history of Manchester United – the first goal for the club by the late, great George Best. He would score more than 170 goals in his United career.

Burnley came out firing in the second half, and, just as in the first, came close to scoring three times and had a credible claim for a penalty turned down, before United made the game safe with a fourth on 68 minutes. Elder, with time to clear, dithered on the ball and lost possession to Charlton, who set up Moore, to score a simple goal. This was followed two minutes later by a fifth, scored by David Herd after a pass from Crerand beat the defensive cover.

Lochhead got a consolation for Burnley three minutes from time when he intercepted a high back-pass from Setters to head home. But it was too little too late, as United won 5-1, exacting revenge for their Boxing Day defeat at Turf Moor.

CLARETS' YEAR ENDS ON UNHAPPY NOTE

United's task made easier by defensive slips

By KEITH McNEE

Manchester United (3), 5; Burnley (0), 1.

MANCHESTER UNITED had the last laugh at Old Trafford on Saturday, gaining ample revenge for that 6—1 Boxing Day defeat at Turf Moor. They were three goals ahead after 25 minutes, through Herd, Moore and Best, and added two more in the second half, Moore and Herd each netting again before Lochhead scored a last minute consolation goal for the Clarets.

This was Burnley's fourth successive defeat in away games, following setbacks against Tottenham, Liverpool and Sheffield Wednesday.

United were worthy winners, but this was a day on which little went right for Burnley from the moment Towers and Harris—forwards who played so well in the Boxing Day match—both failed fitness tests. They were badly missed.

United were worthy winners, but, attack, too, but these were made voluntarily. Quixall and Brennan, ineffective wingers at Turf Moor, were dropped and in came

MAN OF THE MATCH

BOBBY CHARLTON, who didn't score, but was the general of United's rejuvenated attack. Far more effective at centre-forward than in previous games against Burnley on the wing, this display made it easy to see why he is one of the biggest individual box-office attractions in football.

The Press gave Bobby Charlton 'Man of the Match' as Manchester United exacted revenge upon Burnley.

The *Burnley Express* reported that it was a fixture to forget for the Clarets as they did not take their early chances and made many mistakes at the back.

George Best was a real handful that day. Playing on the right wing, he tormented the Burnley defence, Elder in particular, giving the Burnley left-back a miserable time all afternoon, in front of 47,834 lucky souls inside Old Trafford. It was obvious to those present that he was destined for a great future.

Best was a genius of a footballer in his pomp, and is probably the most written about and documented British footballer of all time, on both the front and back pages.

PLAYER PROFILE
Andrew Lorimar Lochhead

Born in Milngavie, near Glasgow, on 9 March 1941, Lochhead was spotted by Burnley scout Jimmy Stein whilst playing for Renfrew Juniors, and he was duly invited by Scotsman Stein for a trial at Turf Moor. The trial proved successful and Lochhead joined the Clarets in 1958, as a 17-year-old. Prior to joining Burnley, Lochhead had a trial at Sunderland but the Rokerites declined to offer him a contract.

Burnley were still 18 months away from winning the First Division title in 1959/60 and young Andy had to learn his craft as a professional player in the reserves during that period, but he impressed the staff as one for the future.

His debut for Burnley came the season after the title win. Lochhead, still a teenager, played in the 1-3 reverse against Manchester City on 30 August 1960.

Sadly for Andy, his next league appearance was not until March 1961, when Burnley played a weakened team (for which they were fined) at home to Chelsea, as they had more pressing matters coming up in the next seven days – a European Cup quarter-final, second-leg tie away at SV Hamburg and an FA Cup semi-final clash versus Tottenham at Villa Park.

Lochhead at Burnley FC.

Lochhead scored twice in the 4-4 draw with Chelsea, and his scoring record, which would eventually lead to over 100 top-flight goals, was up and running.

For the remainder of that season, and the following, he made spasmodic appearances for the first team, although he was top scorer for the reserves as Burnley won the Central League, indicative of the strength of playing staff at the club at this point in time.

Lochhead in action for Burnley.

That was to change in 1962/63 when Lochhead replaced Robson seven fixtures in, joining McIlroy and Pointer in a formidable Burnley attack. Burnley finished third that season and Lochhead was leading scorer with 19 goals. He wasn't quite so prolific in 1963/64, as the Clarets slipped to ninth, but he still led the list of scorers for the second consecutive season. The highlight was obviously the four goals against Manchester United.

From the start of 1964/65 he formed a successful partnership with Irishman Willie Irvine, scoring 43 between them in a mid-table finish, including five versus Chelsea in the last game of the season, when the Londoners fielded a weakened side due to eight players being sent home after breaking a curfew.

Burnley once again competed for the First Division title in 1965/66 (finishing third), with Lochhead netting 15 in the league. He also scored five against Bournemouth in the FA Cup third-round replay, as Burnley romped home 7-0 against the Third Division outfit.

Lochhead reached 100 top-flight league goals at the end of the 1967/68 season but lost his place early in 1968/69 after Burnley lost 4-0 to Liverpool. Without him, the team won their next eight games on the trot. As a result, Lochhead left for Leicester City in late October 1968, making his debut for the Foxes away at Newcastle on 2 November.

As a proven Division One goalscorer, the transfer was a little surprising as Leicester had started badly that season and were languishing in the bottom two. Andy was signed to play alongside record-buy Allan Clarke; however, they were unable to save the Foxes from relegation, although they did play their part in Leicester's run to the FA Cup Final at Wembley, losing by a single goal to Manchester City. Sadly for Leicester City and Lochhead, a presentable chance to win some silverware was lost.

Included within this run was perhaps his most famous goal for Leicester – the headed winner at Anfield in a fifth-round FA Cup replay, when the Foxes beat Liverpool after Peter Shilton had saved a penalty at the Kop End.

Following relegation, Lochhead only played a handful of games for Leicester in the Second Division, and so, after 18 months at Filbert Street, he left for Aston Villa during season 1969/70. However, for the second time running, Lochhead had joined a club during a relegation season, as Villa finished bottom-but-one in Division Two. Fortunately for Lochhead his fortunes soon turned as Villa reached the League Cup Final in 1971 (losing 2-0 to Spurs), before winning promotion back to Division Two in 1971/72.

Lochhead spent three pleasurable years at Villa Park, enjoying cult-hero status as the club experienced an upturn in fortunes following a slump that had taken them to Division Three.

Lochhead wound down his career with time at Oldham Athletic, where he won a Third Division title, followed by a brief spell in the North American Soccer League with Denver Dynamos.

Lochhead at Aston Villa.

It was a mystery why he was never selected for Scotland, but he seemed to have been behind players such as Law, St John, Gilzean and Young. In the modern era, scoring over 100 top-flight goals would make selection almost a certainty, with respect to the current Scottish national team.

Lochhead was a potent striker with a powerful shot and great ability in the air. He was deceptively agile on the ground and had excellent technique. He was more than just a goalscorer.

Numerous defenders have reported since that they tried to kick Lochhead early on in the game to nullify his effectiveness. However, they soon gave up that tactic when he returned the favour even harder, in an era when you could do that.

Andy Lochhead's career numbers are impressive – 159 goals in 466 appearances over a 14-year professional career.

After retiring from football, Lochhead spent 20 years in the licensed trade in Burnley. Nowadays, he can be found back at his beloved Turf Moor, where, aged 78, he is a popular VIP host at Burnley's Premier League fixtures – no doubt with many a story to tell of a different era.

PLAYER PROFILE
William Morgan

Born in Alloa, Scotland, on 2 October 1944, Willie Morgan is considered by many as one of the greatest and most naturally talented players in the history of Burnley Football Club.

Morgan actually had two spells at Burnley, with almost 13 years between his first appearance (April 1963) and his last (January 1976). He played a significant part in the success of the club in the early to mid-60s, before his big money move to Manchester United in 1968. He played until he was 37 years old, making over 600 appearances in English football.

A young Willie Morgan at Burnley.

A prodigious, talented youth footballer, Morgan played as a right-winger and had his pick of clubs to join aged 16. He chose Burnley for his first trial (over Chelsea) in 1960; however, he broke a bone on the day, spending the next six weeks in plaster. He remained in Burnley during his recuperation period, and was so impressed by the club, its staff, the area and the people that he decided to stay. His signing was considered a great coup for the club, even though Burnley were the current league champions.

He initially signed amateur forms, becoming a professional in October 1962 upon his 18th birthday. He did struggle initially to establish himself in the team, due to the playing talent at the club.

England player John Connelly (a member of the 1966 World Cup squad) was the regular right-winger so young Willie had to wait his turn.

Willie Morgan was a good-looking young man, grew his hair fashionably long and became the first footballer to have his own dedicated fan club, developing a sizeable female following as a result.

He made his first-team debut as an 18-year-old in April 1963, versus Sheffield Wednesday at Hillsborough, and immediately impressed with his ability and confidence. By the start of the 1963/64 season, Morgan had become a first-team regular, forcing Connelly to play on the left wing.

The two goals scored against Manchester United on Boxing Day were his first for Burnley, but he was much more of a provider than a consistent goalscorer. The *Clarets Mad* website indicates that Willie had excellent close control, could beat a defender with ease and was a superb crosser of a football, especially onto the forehead of Andy Lochhead. Whilst at Burnley, he was considered to be one of the best wingers in the league.

His consistency inevitably led to a Scottish call-up, becoming just the third Burnley player to represent Scotland when he made his debut versus Northern Ireland at Belfast in 1967. He was also called up to the Scottish squad for the 1974 World Cup in Germany, which was considered to be one of the strongest Scottish teams in its history.

Morgan's style of play and entertaining persona helped him become a Turf Moor favourite, but it became inevitable that he would leave Burnley. By 1968, a young player named Dave Thomas was considered good enough to replace Willie, so he left for Old Trafford for a fee of £117,000. At one point he looked likely to move to Leeds, but the Burnley chairman – Bob Lord, a local butcher – was in dispute with

Leeds United at the time. He therefore pulled the plug on that move, causing a fall-out between himself and Willie Morgan – not for the first time and not for the last!

Morgan's autobiography (*On The Wing* – Trinity Sports Media) outlines that Leeds manager Don Revie had tapped him up with a 'sweetener' of £15,000 to join them, but Mr Lord had already turned down the transfer fee offer of £70,000. Although Morgan confirms that he was transferred to Manchester United somewhat against his will, his wages increased from £130 per week to £165 per week – considered to be the highest wage in English football at that time.

It was a good time to join Manchester United as they had won the league twice in the mid-60s and been crowned European club champions after overcoming Benfica 4-1 in an emotional evening at Wembley in 1968, just ten years after the Munich disaster. Despite this, it was recognised that United's squad needed refreshing, especially in light of George Best beginning to develop a habit for going AWOL.

Morgan joined an attacking line-up that included Kidd, Law, Charlton and Best. Not surprisingly, he became another fans' favourite on the bigger stage at Old Trafford.

Willie Morgan in action for Manchester United.

An ageing United team were relegated in 1974; however, in the following season, Morgan helped United bounce back at the first time of asking in a hugely enjoyable season in Division Two under manager Tommy Docherty. One highlight of Morgan's season would have been his goal in United's victory against First Division Burnley in the League Cup.

Tommy Docherty was ultimately sacked by Manchester United for breach of contract for having a relationship with the wife of the first-team physio (a relationship that still thrives to this day as 'The Doc' went on to marry the lady).

Unfortunately for Morgan, he became involved in a court case when Docherty sued both him and Denis Law for making derogatory comments on regional television about his managerial style. The proceedings unusually made it all the way to court and could have been financially crippling for Willie Morgan had he lost, but the trial collapsed on day three after Docherty was questioned in court by Morgan's barrister.

Willie Morgan was transferred back to Burnley for his second spell at Turf Moor in 1975, after he lost his United place to Steve Coppell. However, his relationship with Burnley chairman Mr Lord was still strained and could not be repaired. As such, Morgan only played in 16 games for the Clarets second time around. By the age of 32, he was frozen out at Burnley and fans wondered if his playing days were at an end.

However, he rejuvenated his career at Bolton Wanderers under manager Ian Greaves, spending four happy and successful seasons there. He made over 150 appearances and helped Wanderers win promotion to the First Division in season 1977/78.

Greaves was very flexible with Morgan, allowing him to play each close season in the North American Soccer League for Chicago and Minnesota, where he amassed 85 regular season games over four

Morgan in action for Chicago Sting in 1977 in the NASL.

seasons. Morgan enjoyed both the football and the lifestyle in America, as his career wound down. However, he finished his career with two seasons at Blackpool before calling time on a distinguished career at age 37.

In total, Morgan made 681 appearances, scoring 59 goals, and won 21 Scottish caps between 1967 and 1974, in an era when Scottish football was at its strongest. He was a magnificent player, with a big personality and is fondly regarded at Burnley, Manchester United and Bolton Wanderers.

After his playing days ended, Morgan owned a chain of laundrettes before becoming the CEO of a sports marketing business that arranges golf tournaments.

Now aged 75, Morgan still lives in the Manchester area.

Graham Moore

Born in Hengoed, Wales, on 7 March 1941, Moore was a very talented all-round sportsman, playing football, basketball and rugby union in his native Wales.

He was working at the local Penalta Colliery and playing football for Bargoed YMCA as a 15-year-old when he was spotted by Cardiff City. He joined the Bluebirds as a trainee and developed sufficiently to make his debut at 17, scoring a late equaliser against Brighton in September 1958.

He played a major part the following season, as Cardiff City won promotion to Division One, by scoring one of the most famous goals in the club's history when his goal against Aston Villa secured promotion. Cardiff won that game 1-0 in front of 55,000 shoe-horned spectators at Ninian Park and were to finish the season in second place, behind Villa.

Moore (extreme left) scoring against Aston Villa to secure promotion.

Graham also made his debut for Wales as a teenager, in a Home Championship match against England. Played at Ninian Park on 17 October 1959, Moore took great joy in scoring a late, headed equaliser for his country, after Jimmy Greaves had given England the lead.

The game was spoilt by incessant wind and driving rain, in front of 60,000 spectators, and in truth was a fairly forgettable affair. Moore went on to win 21 caps for Wales over an 11-year period, but that goal was the only one he scored for his country.

Interestingly, Brian Clough was in the England line-up that day, winning his first cap for England, who were without Billy Wright for the first time in 71 fixtures.

Despite their promotion, Cardiff were in financial difficulty and had to sell their prized young asset to Chelsea in December 1961 for £35,000 – a club record at the time. Moore had played 85 times for Cardiff, scoring 23 goals, and was considered one of the best young talents around. He won the Welsh Sportsman of the Year in 1959 and some compared him to Welsh footballing legend Ivor Allchurch – high praise indeed.

Moore arrived in West London with a big reputation to live up to, as the club were in the early stages of a revolution overseen by Tommy Docherty, who was trying to create a young, vibrant, exciting Chelsea team.

Throughout his career, Moore would never be considered as a great goalscorer (in number terms), but he was a scorer of great goals, and his first two for Chelsea, in just his third appearance for the club, were outstanding. Both were scored from distance versus Spurs at White Hart Lane and offered much promise, although Chelsea lost the game 5-2.

Sadly for Moore, he was unable to add to those two goals in the remainder of the season and Chelsea were relegated.

In possession of significant natural talent, Moore was particularly adept at holding the ball up and linking up play. He had a great touch for a big man, which made up for his lack of pace.

Graham Moore making his debut for Manchester United versus Spurs in October 1963, with United winning 4-1.

Moore played in all but six games the following season, wearing the number 10 shirt, as Chelsea stormed back to the top flight, with Moore forming an effective partnership with Barry Bridges and Bobby Tambling.

In the following season, 1963/64, Moore was a first-team regular in the Blues' early games, as Chelsea looked to establish themselves back in the top flight. In November, however, he played his last game for the club, against Birmingham City, and despite scoring twice he lost his place to Frank Upton. Overall, he scored 14 goals in 72 appearances for Chelsea.

Still only 22 years old, but with five seasons of regular first-team football behind him, Graham Moore departed for Manchester United, as Matt Busby continued to rebuild after Munich.

At United, Moore endured a torrid time with injuries, including a serious leg break. As a result he mustered just 18 appearances over two years with the Red Devils. After recovering from the leg break, he struggled to re-establish himself back into the team, which included David Herd, Denis Law and the developing George Best.

He left for Northampton Town for £15,000 in December 1965 after being offered regular football by Dave Bowen (his Welsh team manager). This was not quite the come down it appears, as Northampton were also in Division One after three promotions in four seasons. It was felt that Moore's talent and experience could help the Cobblers stay up. Sadly, it was not to be, as, despite Moore's best efforts, Northampton were relegated back to Division Two. Incredibly, by season 1969/70, they were back in Division Four, to complete their remarkable journey from Division Four to Division One and back in just nine seasons.

Moore left for Charlton Athletic when Northampton were in Division Three, spending three happy seasons at The Valley. Whilst there, he was recalled to the Welsh national team after an absence of three years. Following Charlton, he wound down his career at Doncaster, before becoming a postmaster in Scarborough and then a pub landlord. He spent his retirement living back in South Wales with his wife.

Moore very sadly passed away in 2016, aged 74, but not before witnessing Cardiff City's return to the top flight in 2013. He was delighted to join the remaining 1959/60 team members as they were honoured on the pitch at half-time.

Despite some suggestions that he didn't quite live up to his billing as 'the new golden boy of Welsh football', Moore played for 17 years, scoring 161 goals in 403 games, winning 21 international caps, and played for two of the biggest teams in the land at that time. With a legacy of some outstanding goals for club and country, I put to you that Moore had a very respectable career indeed. Bravo Sir … and Rest In Peace.

PLAYER PROFILE
David George Herd

Born on 15 April 1934 in Hamilton, Lanarkshire, Herd's mother had actually been sent north of the border to give birth to ensure the offspring could play for Scotland if sufficiently talented! David's father, Alex Herd, was a proud Scot who originated from the area and played for Hamilton before moving south.

The family were based in the Manchester area as David's father played for Manchester City from 1933 to 1948 and later for Stockport County. He was part of the first City side to win the league title in 1936/37, but they were bizarrely relegated the following season despite being top goalscorers. David's uncle, Sandy Herd, also played professional football for Heart of Midlothian and was capped for Scotland.

With excellent footballing pedigree within the family, it was inevitable that young David would show the same sufficient talent. Growing up playing street football in the Moss Side area, one of his friends was Dennis Viollet, who would become a future Old Trafford team-mate.

At 15 years old, Herd signed forms with Stockport County, for whom his father was playing at the time. He made his debut against Hartlepool on the final day of the 1950/51 season and scored in what was a memorable day for the family.

Herd had just turned 17 and lined up alongside his 39-year-old father for the one and only time in his career. It is believed to be the first time in the then 60+ years of league football that a father and son lined up together in the same team. David played on the right wing that day, forming a brief partnership with his father, who was in the dotage of his career.

A rare programme of Stockport County versus Hartlepool when father and son, Alex and David Herd, played alongside each other. It is reported that Alex gave his son a formal handshake to celebrate the youngster's goal, although Alex must have been so proud to be on the same pitch as his son in a professional fixture. (photo: Stockport County FC)

David made excellent progress the following season in his preferred position of centre-forward, scoring five goals in 12 games, although a stint of National Service slowed down his progress somewhat.

Clearly his talent was better than the bottom tier and off he went to Arsenal, where he continued to learn his craft, although not before a swap deal had been agreed with Manchester United with a player called Billy McGee. However, at the last minute, McGee chose Lincoln City instead, and it would be another nine years before Herd joined United.

Had that deal succeeded, Herd would have been part of the Busby Babes, and of course the possibility exists that he could have been a victim of the Munich air disaster.

Herd in action at Arsenal.

Herd joined Arsenal in August 1954 for £10,000, but with the Gunners in transition he struggled early on to secure a place in the first team. During his first two seasons at Highbury he only played a handful of fixtures, after making his debut against Leicester City in February 1955.

That situation changed, however, when Cliff Holton was switched from centre-forward to wing-half, allowing Herd to play up front. As a result, Herd scored with regularity in the 1956/57 season (18 goals in 28 appearances), with his strong, low shot being a particular speciality. He would be Arsenal's top scorer in the next four seasons, including an impressive 29 goals in season 1960/61.

However, from that point on Arsenal suffered indifferent form, with Herd being played out of position by manager George Swindon, which Herd resented. Furthermore, Herd was often offered to other clubs, including Huddersfield and Blackburn, in an attempt by Arsenal to secure deals to improve the club's situation. Herd's disillusionment reached a head when he was offered in a part-exchange deal to bring George Eastham to Highbury. Despite his discontent, Herd continued to play for the Gunners, scoring 107 goals in 180 appearances – a very healthy return that continues to secure Herd's position in Arsenal's all-time top-20 goalscorers to this day.

Herd's scoring record, and discontent, alerted Matt Busby, who was rebuilding after Munich, and he finally arrived at Old Trafford in 1961 for £37,000. He more than justified that fee over the next seven seasons and was generally recognised as one of Matt Busby's wiser signings.

Herd in a Manchester United shirt.

Herd arrived at Old Trafford having been the second highest Division One goalscorer (behind Jimmy Greaves) in season 1960/61. He made his debut for the Red Devils in August 1961 against West Ham, but he initially struggled with United's fluid style of play. Herd had to adapt, and with players like Law and Charlton on the staff he had to be patient. Eventually, however, his patience paid off, as Herd would go on to spearhead one of the game's greatest trinities with the aforementioned Denis Law and Bobby Charlton.

Although United struggled in the league in the 'big-freeze' season of 1962/63, finishing in the bottom four partly as a result of their playing style, they had a memorable run in the FA Cup, beating Huddersfield, Aston Villa, Chelsea, Coventry and Southampton at Villa Park in the semi-final, to set up a delayed Wembley final with Leicester City.

United came into the showpiece fixture as underdogs as Leicester had an excellent season, ending fourth in Division One after topping the division with just four games to go. However, the Red Devils memorably won the final 3-1, with David Herd scoring twice – United's first trophy since the Munich disaster.

Thereafter, Herd was a key component in the United side that went on to win the league twice in seasons 1964/65 and 1966/67. However, his best season in terms of goals was the one in between, when he scored 33 goals in 52 appearances, including a hat-trick against Sunderland, with all three goals being scored past different goalkeepers in a 5-0 win.

Although it is fair to say that, with Law and Charlton alongside him, Herd played an understated role in United's renaissance in the early to mid-60s, he was, nevertheless, mightily effective alongside such exalted company. He was 27, and in his pomp was strong and fast, with a powerful shot that had a knack of keeping low. An analysis of Denis Law's goals reveals that many were scored from rebounds following shots by Herd that successive goalkeepers found too hot to handle.

Sadly for David – and typical for many players of that era – a bad leg break in March 1967, whilst in the act of scoring against Leicester City, hampered his career somewhat. After that, Herd was never a United regular again and lost his place in the European Cup Final (versus Benfica at Wembley in May 1968) to 18-year-old Brian Kidd. Herd did receive a winners' medal, however, as he had played in some of the earlier rounds.

And with that, Herd's United career had come to an end, after 145 goals in 265 appearances, which to this day sees him comfortably in the top 20 of United's all-time greatest goalscorers.

Herd netting for Manchester United.

During 1965 Herd invested funds into 'David Herd Motors' based in Manchester, a company that still exists today, serving the community of Urmston. He once lamented, however, that he wouldn't be able to sell any of his cars to United players as their taste was a little more upmarket than what he had in. The business was, and continues to be, however, very successful, albeit now under new management.

After leaving Old Trafford in July 1968, Herd signed for Stoke City, diligently travelling back and forth from Manchester to Stoke every day for training, whilst working in his business in the afternoon. He stayed for

two seasons, scoring 11 goals in 44 appearances, before being released. He ended his playing career with a brief spell with Irish club Waterford, then managed by his friend Shay Brennan.

Herd hard at work in his motor business.

Herd won five caps for Scotland (scoring three times), all whilst playing for Arsenal. His first came against Wales in Cardiff in October 1958, with his last in 1961 versus Czechoslovakia, which Scotland lost 4-0.

Many feel that this is a poor return for such a talented player, but the Scottish team was selected by a committee in those days, with the manager's role being reduced to that of coaching the players. It is bizarre, however, that he was not selected for Scotland whilst playing at United, as he was part of a deadly attack that included fellow Scot Denis Law, something that Herd was reportedly not amused by.

As well as excelling at football, Herd was a good cricketer, playing at minor counties level and then senior club level into his 60s. He also enjoyed golf, playing off a low handicap on Manchester's finest courses. However, he was a 'rubbish cribbage player' according to Nobby Stiles's memoirs!

Herd managed Lincoln City for one season in the early 70s and sowed some of the seeds of success enjoyed by his successor Graham Taylor in taking them from Division Four re-election candidates to promotion hopefuls. However, he decided that the insecurity of management was not for him after being sacked following a row with his chairman.

David Herd at
Sincil Bank,
home of
Lincoln City.

After Lincoln City, Herd returned to Manchester to run his motor business until he sold it in 1998 to fund his retirement. Thereafter, his life centred around playing golf and exercising his love of foreign travel, with Malta being a particular favourite destination.

David Herd was a hugely talented footballer who shone brightly despite the threat of being overshadowed by the stellar stars who surrounded him at Old Trafford at that time. Fortunately, his footballing talent ensured that that was not the case.

His record of 269 goals in 503 career appearances – all bar 15 at the top level – is formidable, with his work rate and commitment being much admired by team-mates, opponents and fans alike. Players like Herd are really appreciated by clubs and fans – hardworking, honest, a team man and, in David's case, a consistent performer and goalscorer.

David sadly passed away in October 2016, aged 82 years old, after a long illness that he fought bravely, and he is much missed by followers of some of the biggest clubs in our land. He was instrumental in the rebuild of Manchester United, following the Munich disaster, into a footballing powerhouse and has a special place in the heart of Red Devils followers of a certain vintage.

Rest In Peace.

Chapter 5

Fulham v Ipswich Town

10 - 1

Kick-off: 3pm   Venue: Craven Cottage   Attendance: 19,374

Macedo	1	Bailey
Cohen	2	Davin
Langley	3	Compton
⚽ Mullery	4	Baxter
Keetch	5	Bolton
⚽ Robson	6	Dougan
Key	7	Broadfoot
⚽ Cook	8	Moran
⚽⚽⚽⚽ Legatt	9	Baker ⚽
Haynes	10	Phillips
⚽⚽⚽ Howfield	11	Blackwood

The Managers
Bedford Jezzard   Jackie Milburn

Match Report

After 23 goals in our first three fixtures, we arrived at Craven Cottage in West London for a match that sent records tumbling with an incredible 11 goals. It was the highest aggregate scoring game of the day and set the following records:

- the largest aggregate score of the season

- the highest individual team score of the season

- the largest winning margin of the season

- the last time a top-flight team scored ten goals in a single game

- the highest scoring Football League game in Fulham's history

- the quickest top-flight hat-trick

Sadly, however, under 20,000 turned up in West London to witness one of the most memorable fixtures in Football League history.

Fulham in 1963.

Ipswich Town.

Contained within the Fulham ranks, and under the stewardship of the extravagantly named Bedford Jezzard, were four players who served their club(s), their country, and the game in general with great distinction:

• George Cohen, who was England's World Cup-winning right-back

• Alan Mullery, who played for England in the 1970 World Cup

• Bobby Robson, who went on to manage both Ipswich Town and England with great distinction

• Johnny Haynes, who was one of the most elegant passing footballers of his generation

Fulham went into the fixture on a five-game unbeaten run but still sat just five places above the relegation zone.

Ipswich, meanwhile, had won the First Division just 18 months previously under Sir Alf Ramsey, just one season after getting promoted. However, Ramsey had left to mastermind the ultimately successful World Cup campaign, leaving Ipswich to play under Jackie Milburn, who had been a legendary player with Newcastle United. In the Ipswich line-up that day was goalkeeper Roy Bailey, whose son Gary would later play for Manchester United, and Gerry Baker, who was making a name for himself as a striker.

Ipswich Town were very poor on their travels that season, winning none, drawing four and losing 17 of their 21 fixtures. In total they conceded 121 goals (76 away from home), leading inevitably to relegation. But even by their standards that season their performance at Fulham on Boxing Day was quite stunning in terms of defensive ineptitude.

Ipswich arrived at Craven Cottage, having won just two of their opening 24 league games, with relegation already a certainty. They'd conceded 58 goals, a figure that would more than double by the end of the season, and were bottom of the league at Christmas, a position from which they never recovered.

The *Eastern Daily Press* reported that Milburn was a proper gentleman but had difficulty setting his team up defensively – evidenced by the fact that Ipswich shipped ten in this fixture, nine at Stoke, six at Spurs, Liverpool, Arsenal and Bolton, and seven at home to Manchester United!

On a pudding of a pitch, the contest was fairly even for the first 12 minutes, and could easily have been 2-2, with George Dougan hitting the post twice for Ipswich. However, Fulham started to dominate the game thereafter, with the game exploding into life on the quarter-hour mark when Fulham opened the scoring.

Johnny Key crossed from the right and Cook connected with a diving header at the far post. Incredibly, the game was over as a contest just five minutes later as Fulham went 4-0 up when Graham Leggat scored one of the quickest hat-tricks in the history of football.

His first goal was a tap-in, following a rebound off the crossbar. His second arrived just 60 seconds later, squeezing in a shot off the post. The third goal, 90 seconds later, was Leggat's best – a powerful shot from 25 yards, giving keeper Bailey no chance.

Game over as a contest after only 20 minutes.

Bobby Howfield made it five shortly before half-time when Bailey flapped at a corner, completely missing the ball, as it flew straight in. Ipswich finally pulled a goal back with the last action of the half through Gerry Baker. Six goals scored in 45 minutes – breathless action for the spectators present, who began speculating as to what the second half would deliver. Surely Ipswich's defence couldn't be quite so profligate?

As it happened, they could.

Just six minutes after the restart, Bobby Howfield scored again with a cross-shot from the left-wing position. Then Bobby Robson netted shortly afterwards, with what was his only goal that season, finishing neatly after Ipswich were cut open once again, and – are you keeping up? – it was 7-1 with over 20 minutes still to go.

Howfield made it 8-1 on 71 minutes, with another effort cutting in from the left, to join Leggat with a hat-trick. Ipswich, at this point, were ragged to say the least and were hoping for the final whistle so they could get back on their team bus and return to Suffolk.

The weather conditions began to worsen, as mist started to roll in off the adjacent River Thames, and the Ipswich defence were left mystified when Alan Mullery scored with a 20-yarder past Bailey for Fulham's ninth.

The final goal of the match was scored late on by the brilliant Leggat from close range to register his fourth of the day, and, incredibly, Fulham's tenth.

**A rare Ipswich Town attack
in the mud at Craven Cottage.**

Ipswich Town keeper Roy Bailey could have been forgiven for developing back problems, having conceded ten goals to Fulham. On this occasion Fulham's Leggat offers to collect the ball for Bailey, after the third of his four goals.

This famous picture was taken by *Mirror* photographer Monty Fresco, who had been at West Ham that morning and so witnessed 21 goals in 180 minutes of football.

The Hammersmith End were heard singing that never-to-be-heard chant in English football, 'We want 11!' However, the final whistle blew soon after, to save Ipswich Town from further embarrassment.

As it did, so the fog descended upon West London, engulfing Craven Cottage in the process – just too late to save Ipswich. They returned home along the A12, having suffered their heaviest defeat in the club's history – with Fulham, not surprisingly, securing their greatest-ever Football League victory.

In more recent times three Premiership teams have scored nine – Manchester United (versus Ipswich Town – sorry Tractor Boys), Tottenham Hotspur (versus Wigan Athletic) and Leicester City (at Southampton). However, this fixture on the banks of the River Thames, some 56 years ago, remains the last time a team scored double figures.

Return Match

Ipswich Town
4-2
Fulham

Date: 28 December   **Venue:** Portman Road   **Att:** 15,808

With the return fixture played just 48 hours later, and with the Christmas holiday period still in full swing, the Ipswich Town match programme obviously had to be printed before the festive period had started. As such, Town fans were greeted with these profound words from manager Jackie Milburn in the opening pages:

'I can only hope that Ipswich kept up the good work against Fulham at Craven Cottage on Boxing Day. I am afraid that these notes had to be completed long before the result of that match was known so I can only keep my fingers crossed.'

Oh dear!

As you might predict, the return fixture followed the pattern of some of the other games, with the club suffering a hiding on Boxing Day, turning the tables on their opponents two days later.

Contrary to their shocking defensive discipline away from Suffolk, Ipswich were actually decent at home in 1963/64. Across the second half of the season they secured three 4-3 home victories – a scoreline that is normally witnessed maybe once in a season, so there was no shortage of excitement at Portman Road for Town fans.

However, their poor defensive record across the whole season, particularly away from home, saw the club relegated to Division Two, despite having won the First Division title just two seasons prior.

The team changes for the return fixture were minimal: Fulham remained unchanged, while Ipswich resisted the temptation to make wholesale changes by making only one – Danny Hegan came in for Ted Phillips.

Baxter got Ipswich off to a decent start with a goal from a set piece on 11 minutes, but the in-form Leggat levelled it up five minutes before the break. Crucially for Town, however, Hegan scored on the cusp of half-time to give the Tractor Boys a 2-1 lead and some confidence going into the break, although, to be fair, Ipswich won nine home fixtures that season and were a different proposition on home soil.

Fulham got their second equaliser on 62 minutes when Johnny Key scored with a shot from the inside-right position and Town fans were perhaps fearing the worst. However, to their eternal credit (having taken a mauling just 48 hours earlier), Ipswich found the energy and determination to score twice in the final ten minutes to win the game 4-2, and, in doing so, winning back some of their pride. Goals from Broadfield and Baker did the trick in front of 15,808 at Portman Road.

There was a similar attendance the following week when Ipswich put six past Oldham Athletic in the FA Cup third round, with three more goals from Baker – plenty of entertainment and goals galore in Suffolk that season.

Despite winning three of their last four league games of the campaign, Ipswich Town were relegated from Division One, finishing bottom of the league, four points adrift of safety, after conceding 121 goals. As such, their title-winning side began to be dismantled but the club did not collapse completely, finishing fifth in the Second Division the following season. They finally gained promotion back to Division One in season 1967/68 as the club began to rebuild, going on to enjoy incredible success during their ten years under Bobby Robson ... who had played for Fulham against them on this particular day!

Fulham ended the 1963/64 season in a lowly 15th position and followed this up with two bottom-three finishes over the next two seasons, narrowly avoiding relegation in the process (only two went down in those days). Unfortunately, their luck ran out in season 1967/68, as they were relegated along with Sheffield United. They went on to be relegated again to Division Three the following season and it would be over 30 years before they climbed back up to the big time – by then called the Premier League.

PLAYER PROFILE
Graham Leggat

Born in Aberdeen on 20 June 1934, Leggat scored over 200 goals in League football either side of the Border and won 18 caps for Scotland. He remains one of Fulham's highest-ever goalscorers in their history, with 127 goals in 254 matches and his contribution to this amazing day is assured.

Leggat at Fulham Football Club.

Graham Leggat joined his home-town club in 1953, whilst also qualifying as a Physical Education teacher, and immediately impressed with his speed and agility. He made his debut aged 18 and helped the Dons reach the Scottish FA Cup Final in 1954 (losing 2-1 to Celtic), thanks to his ability to play anywhere across the forward line.

In 1955 Aberdeen broke the monopoly of the Glasgow giants, winning the Scottish League title for the first time in their history. The following season Leggat scored the decisive goal as the Dons beat St Mirren 2-1 in the League Cup Final. He netted 29 goals in 29 games that season and earned a call-up for Scotland for their game versus England at Hampden Park – the fixture all Scots want to play in. He gained instant hero status when he put Scotland ahead with a cool finish, but future Fulham colleague Johnny Haynes equalised with 90 seconds remaining in front of 132,000 at Hampden Park.

Graham Leggat in a Scotland shirt.

Leggat continued to star for Aberdeen despite some nagging injuries and a leg break in 1957. He regained his fitness to play in the 1958 World Cup held in Sweden, starring in two of Scotland's three fixtures, so it was somewhat of a surprise when Second Division Fulham were successful with a bid of only £17,000 – a fee to be repaid many times over.

Fulham were a high-scoring unit at the time, so Leggat slotted straight in, endearing himself to the Fulham faithful by scoring in his first six games, all won, including a 6-1 demolition of Stoke City. By the end of that season Leggat had scored 21 times as Fulham cantered to promotion in 1958/59. He netted 18 goals the following season as Fulham finished comfortably in mid-table, including a treble in a 3-3 thriller at Old Trafford and four in a 5-0 thumping of Leeds United.

Fulham struggled thereafter, finishing in the bottom third for a few seasons, but Leggat's personal contribution remained high, averaging 15 goals a season. Leggat almost helped Fulham to the 1961/62 FA Cup Final, scoring the opening goal in their semi-final 1-1 draw against Burnley at Villa Park before a 68,000-strong crowd. However, Burnley prevailed

2-1 in the replay at Filbert Street, but not before Fulham were on the wrong side of a controversial decision when they should have been awarded a late penalty.

Over the next four seasons from 1962 to 1966, Fulham survived in Division One, with Leggat making telling contributions, including goals against Arsenal and Liverpool, and remaining a crucial component in the team despite now being the wrong side of 30.

By now, however, he was no longer a regular, despite scoring when recalled – including a hat-trick versus Leicester at Christmas and a brace versus Stoke on New Year's Eve. Fulham stayed up again but he was inexplicably sold to Birmingham days later and the general view from 'the Hammersmith End' was that it was too early for Leggat to go, bringing a sad end to his eight-year Fulham career. He remains the only Fulham player to have scored 100 goals in the top flight of English football.

Leggat scoring past Gordon Banks for Fulham against Leicester in December 1966. Leggat netted a hat-trick that day as Fulham won 4-2, but he was in his final knockings of his Fulham career by then.

A fantastic tribute by Aberdeen fans.

Leggat did not enjoy success at either Birmingham City (scoring just three times) or Rotherham United (scoring just seven times) whom he joined after just one season at St Andrew's. After a brief stint with non-league Bromsgrove Rovers in 1970, he retired from English football.

After scoring 201 goals in 395 fixtures, Leggat coached the Toronto Metros in Canada from 1971, before moving into writing and broadcasting, becoming a well-known face on Canadian TV talking about football.

Graham sadly passed away in Toronto in August 2015 aged 81 after enjoying a great career on both sides of the border.

Well done Sir and Rest In Peace.

Robert Michael Howfield

Born in Watford, Hertfordshire, on 3 December 1936, Bobby Howfield had a remarkable sports career, making a living as a professional athlete in two different sports in two different countries, which is extremely rare.

Howfield showed great promise as a youth footballer with his strong shot being a particular strength. At 17 years old he played for his local side Bushey United before being spotted by his nearest league side Watford, who soon offered him terms. He developed through their junior teams, finally making his senior debut in season 1957/58. In two seasons he made 47 appearances, scoring nine goals before moving north to sign for Crewe Alexandra in the summer of 1959.

He failed to settle there, making just five appearances at Gresty Road before returning south to join Aldershot three months later for a fee of £1,500. He did well with the Shots in his first season, top scoring with 14 goals.

Aldershot in spring 1962 at their famous ground set in a public park. Bobby Howfield is on the far right, front row.

Howfield suffered misfortune at the beginning of the 1960/61 season when, after scoring twice in a game against Barrow, he broke his leg badly, which side-lined him for the rest of that season. He was back to his sparky best though in 1961/62, racking up 23 goals to become a fans' favourite. However, his relationship with club management was not so good, with Howfield reported as being a tad temperamental. After a number of warnings about his attitude, he was suspended in March 1962 for missing training and arriving late for a fixture.

After 76 appearances and 44 goals for Aldershot – mostly powerful shots – Howfield decided he would only sign a month-by-month contract for season 1962/63. Thus, when Watford showed an interest in their former player, the Aldershot hierarchy accepted a bid of £4,000.

Howfield's second spell at Vicarage Road lasted 15 months, with 15 goals being scored in 45 appearances before stepping up to join First Division Fulham for £6,000 in November 1963 – just before the Boxing Day fixture in which he scored a memorable hat-trick in Fulham's 10-1 win.

Howfield in action for Fulham, ending up in the net against West Bromwich Albion.

Howfield's stay at Craven Cottage only lasted until the end of the following season because he wasn't always an automatic choice, as the step up in quality was evident, although he still notched nine goals in 26 appearances.

New Aldershot manager, Dave Smith, had one eye on Howfield's crowd-pulling potential when he took over the Shots in August 1965 and persuaded Howfield to return. He stayed for two more seasons, scoring ten goals in 34 appearances, but once again Howfield was continually in conflict with management and was served a number of suspensions for breaches of club discipline before being released in the summer of 1967.

At around this time Howfield entered a 'Kicking Clinic' held in the UK, and his prowess led to further trials in the United States, with him being subsequently signed by the National Football league Denver Broncos as a kicker.

For those unfamiliar with American football, kickers start the action by kicking-off, restart the game and convert field goals and conversions – an integral part of any NFL side.

He kicked for Denver with distinction for three seasons (1968–1970) before being traded to the New York Jets where he stayed for four more seasons. The best afternoon of his NFL career came in 1972 when he kicked six field goals to lift the Jets to an 18-17 victory over New Orleans. The final kick came as time expired. He termed it 'my biggest thrill since coming to the United States.'

In 1974, Howfield became a US citizen, before retiring from professional sport at 38 years old, after suffering a few injuries during that year. He loved the lifestyle in America and was able to indulge in his passion for sports cars. Several years later, in 1991, Bobby's son Ian followed in his father's footsteps into American football by joining the Houston Oilers, also as a kicker.

OGUARD62'S 1969 REPLAY

Monday, January 5, 1970   *"The preferred source for APBA Football news."*   Morning Edition

BRONCOS WIN FIRST AFL CROWN AS TIME EXPIRED

At Mile High Stadium attendance 50,583. Bill Thompson's 50-yard kick return setup Bobby Howfield's 40-yard field goal as the gun went off. Floyd Little rushed for 151 yards on 16 carries. Denver had a plus 4 turnover advantage. Bobby Howfield made of 5 field goals.

Bobby Howfield - File Photo

New York (8-8-0)	0	7	0	9 - 16
Denver (11-4-1)	7	3	3	6 - 19

Den - Embree 26 pass from Tensi (Howfield kick)
NY - Mathis 11 pass from Namath (J. Turner kick)
Den - FG Howfield 16
Den - FG Howfield 24
NY - FG J. Turner 29, 12:23
NY - FG J. Turner 41, 9:33
Den - FG Howfield 21, 4:46
NY - FG J. Turner 24, 1:21
Den - FG Howfield 40, 0:00

Having made headlines on the banks of the River Thames, Howfield made them in Denver and in New York.

Howfield had an interesting career on both sides of the Atlantic and used his talent for kicking a ball to good effect, leaving behind many memories for fans of many different sports clubs. In total, he played for ten years as a professional in England (233 appearances, 85 goals) and seven years with NFL teams (487 points in 89 appearances, with 98 field goals).

After his playing days were over he worked in the insurance department of a Denver bank and now, aged 83, he still resides in that area.

Howfield in action for the New York Jets.

Chapter 6

Leicester City v Everton

2 - 0

Kick-off: 3pm   **Venue: Filbert Street**   **Attendance: 30,004**

Banks	1	Rankin
Chalmers	2	Brown
Norman	3	Harris
McLintock	4	Gabriel
King	5	Heslop
Appleton	6	Kay
Riley	7	Scott
Cross	8	Stevens
⚽⚽ Keyworth	9	Young
Gibson	10	Vernon
Stringfellow	11	Temple

The Managers
Matt Gillies   Harry Catterick

Match Report

In true parliamentary fashion, I must first register an interest in Leicester City. My first visit to Filbert Street was as a nine-year-old in November 1965 and I have missed very few home fixtures in the 55 years since. I therefore marginally missed this fixture, despite almost certainly asking if I could go, especially as it was Christmas holiday time, meaning no school the following day. However, my father would have told me that I was still too young, thus delaying my inauguration as a Foxes fan for another 22 months.

If I had attended this fixture, I would have witnessed the most 'normal' result of the day. Had *Match of the Day* been operating in 1963 as it is today (i.e. showing every fixture), then it is highly likely that it would have been last in the running order.

This was a fixture between two of the previous season's top-four teams (Everton were champions) and both would go on to finish in the top half of the table again. The Toffees finished third this time, thanks to some legendary Evertonians in their ranks, including Scot Alex Young (275 Everton appearances, 89 goals) and Welshman Roy Vernon, with the pair forming an excellent partnership.

To this day, Young is remembered by many Evertonians as 'the golden vision'. Vernon, meanwhile, was an outstanding footballer, but he had a consistent record of challenging authority wherever he played. He left Blackburn after one row too many, and after joining Everton he soon clashed with new manager Catterick when he assumed the reins at Goodison by being sent home from a tour after breaking a curfew. However, Catterick could see his quality and made Young captain to try and keep him onside.

Alex Young at Everton in 1963.

Young's strike partner Roy Vernon was a heavy smoker who often lit up in the tunnel just before and just after games and was proud of his technique of taking a shower without getting his cigarette wet! However, Catterick eventually got fed up with his antics and sold him to Stoke City in 1965.

The Everton line-up on this Boxing Day also included Derek Temple, who was to score the

Everton in 1963.

winner in the 1966 FA Cup Final some 30 months later after Everton were 2-0 down against Sheffield Wednesday.

Everton were backed by Littlewoods Pools owners the Moores family, with funds being made available to sign quality players from the early 60s. The club were often referred to as the 'Mersey Millionaires', with John Moores being fiercely ambitious for success. So much so, in fact, that he sacked popular manager Johnny Carey in March 1961 in the back of a taxi! Carey and Moores were going to a meeting and Carey asked for clarification of his position following a losing run of seven games after being second in the table in the 1960/61 season. 'You are sacked,' was Moores's reply, and this was the origin of the phrase 'Taxi for ...' if a supporter base wanted a manager dismissed.

Carey's replacement was former Evertonian Harry Catterick, who had worked wonders on a limited budget at Sheffield Wednesday and was a strict disciplinarian. He had a room under the stand at Goodison Park where under-performing or ill-disciplined players were summoned for some 'counselling', often keeping the players waiting for added effect. Not surprisingly, this room became known as the 'Bollocking Room'.

However, Catterick's strict approach to discipline worked and Everton became one of the powerhouses of the 1960s: league champions in season 1962/63, FA Cup winners in 1966, finalists in 1968 (losing in extra time to a Jeff Astle goal for West Bromwich Albion) and champions again in 1969/70, with a midfield of Colin Harvey, Alan Ball and Howard Kendall, who many Evertonians regard as their best ever. In short, if you played against Everton in the 1960s you knew that it was going to be a tough fixture.

This was the era when attacking players regularly got the better of defenders and there were 20 goals in Everton's first four fixtures that season, which included a 5-1 defeat at Old Trafford and losing by the odd goal in a seven-goal thriller at Burnley.

Leicester City in 1963/1964

Everton were sitting in eighth position that Boxing Day morning and came into the fixture on a high, having exacted revenge on Manchester United by beating them 4-0 at Goodison Park just five days previously. However, they were a little depleted, being without Morgan, Parker and Labone; thus, Leicester's performance and win should be viewed with a degree of context.

Leicester were also a decent team back then, almost winning the domestic double in the previous season. They were top of the league as late as 16 April after beating Manchester United 4-3, with a hat-trick from Ken Keyworth. Called the 'Ice Kings' and with a unique playing style involving inter-changeable players Graham Cross and Frank McLintock, and an effective left-flank threat through Davie Gibson and Mike Stringfellow, the Foxes lost just once at home all season and played through the coldest winter in many years. With just four fixtures to go, they were top of the table and in the cup final, where they were favourites to beat Manchester United, who were to finish 19th that season. Sadly, though, Leicester failed to win any of their final games (all away due to the backlog of fixtures), ending the season in fourth. To compound the misery for Foxes fans, they also lost the FA Cup Final 3-1 to a Denis Law-inspired Red Devils team.

So with Everton defending the title (their sixth) and Leicester City looking to compete strongly again, this was a much-anticipated fixture in front of 30,004 at Filbert Street. The club's first 30,000+ gate of the season was achieved despite the fixture clashing with Leicester Tigers' rugby union game versus the Barbarians RFC at Welford Road (just 200 yards from Filbert Street), which also attracted a large gate, being the club's traditional holiday showpiece game.

Despite conditions being really tricky with 'a couple of inches of slime on top of a rock-hard surface' (quote from the *Leicester Mercury*), Leicester coped better with some crisp passing and tighter defensive discipline.

BEST HOME PERFORMANCE OF THE SEASON

A Slick City Had Everton On The Slide

FIRST DIVISION champions Everton were outclassed at Filbert Street yesterday by a Leicester City side far more superior than the 2-0 final score suggests.

So much were the Merseysiders reduced to playing second fiddle that England 'keeper Gordon Banks did not have his first test until the 37th minute and in all had only three spots of bother with which to deal.

During the interval a crowd of the fans broke into song. "Bless 'em all" was the chosen verse and it pretty well sums up my reaction to a first class entertainment.

As was the case when Harry Catterick's men crashed at City HQ last season this was a victory for football.

By Laurie Simpkin

And as the headline on the right confirms, it was one of the best Leicester City performances of the season, with the 2-0 scoreline flattering Everton. England's 1966 World Cup-winning goalkeeper Gordon Banks – who had by now established himself as a quality First Division custodian and had earned a number of England caps – was not tested by Everton until the 37th minute, and in truth was only called upon three times over the whole game, such was Leicester's dominance.

It was to be Ken Keyworth's fixture as he scored both goals for Leicester. His first came on 30 minutes when great play by Frank McLintock and Davie Gibson found Mike Stringfellow, who turned the ball into the area for Keyworth to finish smartly from close range.

Gibson and Stringfellow played together on Leicester's left flank for nine seasons and seemed to have an instinctive partnership that served Leicester well, and they are often regarded as being two of Leicester's top-20 players of all time. In fact, my father Bill Davidson, who was a regular at Leicester City fixtures from 1955 to his passing in 2002, rated Davie Gibson as his best-ever player.

Although Kay of Everton nearly levelled when Vernon put him through, Banks was able to smother his shot on 37 minutes and it was 1-0 at half-time.

On the hour mark, Leicester gave themselves some breathing space when Appleton found Gibson on the left and his low cross found Keyworth, who once again beat Rankin in the Everton goal. Everton were never really in the game from that point on, and McLintock came close to scoring a third for Leicester on a couple of occasions, but Rankin denied him. Leicester saw out the game comfortably to secure a fine 2-0 victory against the current Division One champions.

Patrons leaving the fixture could have been forgiven for thinking that Leicester City's victory, in beating the powerhouse Everton team, may have been the footballing story of the day. However, on a day of explosive fixtures and scorelines, this was instead a solid, normal, high-quality Division One match, won by the team who coped better with the conditions and who passed the ball better.

Leicester's hero was two-goal Ken Keyworth – one of the, perhaps, more low-key heroes of Boxing Day 1963.

Return Match

Everton
0-3
Leicester City

Date: 28 December   **Venue:** Goodison Park   **Att:** 54,808

The teams travelled north to Goodison Park on the train to play the return fixture some 48 hours later in front of 54,808, with Leicester going one better by winning three goals to nil. The scoreline meant Everton became the only team to draw a scoring blank over the festive period. Bearing in mind Everton's quality and the fact that they went on to finish third that season, these results for Leicester were very impressive and were almost certainly their finest two victories of the season.

Both teams made one change – Everton replaced Kay with Morgan to complete a defensive re-shuffle, whilst Leicester's hero from Boxing Day, Keyworth, had taken a blow to his knee and failed his fitness test, a test that, according to the *Leicester Mercury*, consisted of a 'brisk walk'! Keyworth was replaced by young Scot Bobby Roberts, who was not really an attacking player but operated a little more defensively.

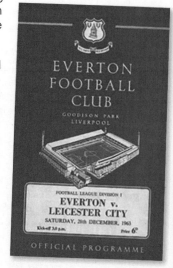

The match report from the day indicated that the referee (Mr Fussey from Retford – yes really!) lost a little control, with physical battles being fought all over the place. However, Leicester kept their nerve and discipline to win 3-0, with goals from Stringfellow and two from Bobby Roberts either side of half-time – his first ever Division One goals.

BOBBY'S A DAZZLER!
Two Goals Crown A
Fine Display

SCOREBOARD
EVERTON 0
CITY - - - 3

STRINGFELLOW (City)
ROBERTS (City) 86 minutes
ROBERTS (City) 85 minutes

Official attendance · 36,000

LEICESTER CITY CERTAINLY SEEM TO HAVE THE MERSEY BEAT. THEIR WELL EARNED WIN AT GOODISON THIS AFTERNOON GAVE THEM THE DOUBLE OVER THE CHAMPIONS, EVERTON, AND THEIR THIRD SUCCESS AGAINST A MERSEY TEAM THIS TERM.

* * *

The match was one which Bobby Roberts will long remember. He scored his first...

After those disappointing couple of results, Everton then went on a run of 12 unbeaten games (nine wins, three draws, scoring 33 goals) that catapulted them up the table. Their run featured a 3-1 home win versus eventual champions Liverpool, with 66,515 shoe-horned into Goodison Park, along with a 6-1 home win versus Nottingham Forest in front of another gate north of 50,000.

However, Everton lost three of their last five fixtures to finish third – just one point off second placed Manchester United. Everton had signed Fred Pickering from Blackburn Rovers in March 1964 for a British record fee of £85,000, and, although he scored a hat-trick on his debut versus Nottingham Forest, Everton were unable to catch their Merseyside rivals that season.

As for Leicester, the 1963/64 season offered much promise and optimism, and a 7-2 win, early in the season at home to Arsenal, confirmed their talent. However, inconsistency and too many draws hampered their progress somewhat and they were unable to repeat the previous season's heroics, eventually finishing the season in 11th spot. There were some successes though, including winning at Anfield versus the eventual champions and lifting the League Cup later that season by beating Stoke City over two legs – their first major trophy in their 80-year history. Justifiable reward indeed for a talented group of players.

That, however, was as good as it got for Leicester City in the 1960s. They finished 11th, 18th, seventh, eighth and 13th between 1963 and 1968, before being relegated in season 1968/69, despite spending an English record transfer fee of £150,000 on Allan Clarke in the summer of 1968 and reaching the FA Cup Final that same season. The downward spiral saw long-serving manager Matt Gillies sacked after a 7-1 defeat in November 1968 at ... Everton!

PLAYER PROFILE
Kenneth Keyworth

Born in Rotherham on 24 February 1934, Keyworth was an amateur with Wolves before signing for his local team Rotherham United in January 1952 after completing his National Service, aged almost 18 years old.

He was picked up by Leicester City at the end of the 1957/58 season after impressing at Millmoor, albeit as a wing-half, making 87 appearances and scoring six goals.

At Leicester he was converted into a more forward-thinking player, becoming a consistent goalscorer over seven seasons, with all of his 177 League appearances being in the First Division (215 appearances in all competitions, scoring 77 goals in total). He was the club's top scorer for three consecutive seasons from 1961/62. He played in two FA Cup finals – 1961 and 1963 – scoring in the 1963 final with an instinctive diving header.

Without being disrespectful, Keyworth was often described as an honest grafter, a rugged and unselfish footballer – not very flashy but quietly effective.

He was perfect for that era and entirely consistent with his county of birth. Every club needs that type of player – one who squeezes every drop out of their natural talent, works hard and rarely causes a problem.

Sadly his career was somewhat curtailed by a serious car crash that limited his effectiveness and his career fizzled out with brief spells at Coventry City and Swindon Town.

A Division One goal ratio of 63 in 177 games (one goal per 2.8 games – not too far off Jamie Vardy's record, to give some modern context) is not to be sniffed at, however, and Keyworth is remembered fondly by Foxes fans as being an integral part of the exciting Leicester City team of the early 1960s.

After his playing days ended, Keyworth returned to Rotherham and became a quantity surveyor.

Sadly, Keyworth passed away on 7 January 2000 aged 65 and remains one of only two members of a very exclusive club – those who have scored for Leicester City in an FA Cup Final. There have been no further applications for membership of that group since 1963, and all readers of a Leicester City persuasion can be eternally hopeful that that exclusive two-some will extend its membership sometime soon.

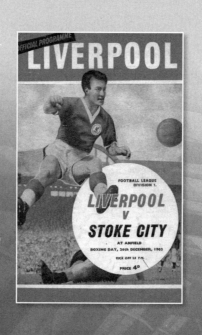

Chapter 7

Liverpool v Stoke City

6 - 1

Kick-off: 3pm   **Venue: Anfield**   **Attendance: 49,942**

Lawrence	1	Leslie
Ferns	2	Asprey
Moran	3	Allen
Milne	4	Palmer
Yeats	5	Stuart
Stevenson	6	Skeels
Callaghan	7	Viollet
⚽⚽⚽⚽ Hunt	8	Kinnell
⚽ St John	9	Ritchie ⚽
⚽ Arrowsmith	10	Dobing
Thompson	11	Bebbington

The Managers
Bill Shankly   Tony Waddington

Match Report

After the relative normality of Leicester City versus Everton, Anfield was the venue for a sensational fixture, full of drama, goals and a player scoring four.

Stoke City had been promoted the previous season and were enjoying life off the field too as a newly promoted club by proudly marketing their club to potential (new) fans in the satellite towns in Staffordshire (Lichfield, Stone, Uttoxeter, Stafford etc) with the flyer opposite.

In the pre-universal motorway days, and before the rail network was trimmed significantly by Dr Beeching in 1969, rail was the preferred mode of transport for many fans not living locally.

Perhaps not surprisingly, Stoke struggled a little on the pitch after promotion. They began the fixture just above the drop zone in 18th position (eventually finishing in 17th), having lost their last three games. Although they had started the season with two wins against Tottenham Hotspur and Aston Villa, they did not win again until their 13th game on 2 October, when they won 4-3 at Bolton, with striker John Ritchie (signed from non-league football 18 months previously) scoring twice – the first of six consecutive league games in which he scored.

Also pre-Christmas were two dramatic 4-4 draws at the Victoria Ground versus Burnley and Sheffield Wednesday, with Ritchie scoring five of the eight goals. And that's what saved Stoke that season – scoring goals. They notched 77 in total – only the top eight scored more – which helped them pick up points despite a leaky defence.

For Liverpool this was the first Christmas since Beatlemania and an additional unstoppable movement was developing on Merseyside – a great Liverpool football team under their iconic manager Bill Shankly. This victory was one of 16 home wins that season (bizarrely, no draws) that propelled the Reds to their first top-flight title since 1947.

They too had a bizarre start to the season, losing their first three home fixtures to Nottingham Forest, Blackpool and West Ham, but winning three of their first four away games. The home hoodoo was settled when they put six past Wolves on 16 September, but Blackburn won at Anfield on 14 December to leave the Reds in fourth place coming into the Stoke game.

FIRST DIVISION FOOTBALL
AT STOKE

SEASON 1963/64

SPECIAL TRAINS TO

STOKE

FOR SATURDAY FIXTURES

Date		Opponents
1963—		
24th August	...	TOTTENHAM HOTSPUR
7th September	...	LEICESTER CITY
14th September	...	NOTTINGHAM FOREST
28th September	...	BLACKPOOL
19th October	...	FULHAM
2nd November	...	BURNLEY
16th November	...	SHEFFIELD WEDNESDAY
30th November	...	BIRMINGHAM CITY
21st December	...	WOLVERHAMPTON WANDERERS
28th December	...	LIVERPOOL
1964—		
1st February	...	BLACKBURN ROVERS
15th February	...	CHELSEA
22nd February	...	BOLTON WANDERERS
7th March	...	WEST BROMWICH ALBION
21st March	...	IPSWICH TOWN
4th April	...	EVERTON
18th April	...	MANCHESTER UNITED

Kick-off times for these matches will be 3.15 pm

Passengers from Stations, other than those served by the special trains
shown overleaf, should enquire at their local station for details of services
to and from Stoke.

Liverpool (in their famous red with white shorts) were without Jimmy Melia, so in came Ian St John at inside-left. In front of almost 50,000, on a greasy, tricky pitch, Liverpool struggled initially to get a foothold in the game as Stoke City (wearing white with black shorts) were the better side for much of the first half. They moved the ball nicely, with Peter Dobing especially effective, and were considered unlucky to be only on level terms at half-time.

Ian St John put Liverpool ahead on nine minutes following Peter Thompson's cross, which was flicked on by Roger Hunt to St John, who ducked low to head the ball well wide of Leslie in the Stoke goal, at the Kop End of Anfield.

John Ritchie levelled for Stoke City on 35 minutes when Viollet, Palmer and Kinnell engineered an opening for Ritchie to beat Tommy Lawrence with a powerful shot to the bottom corner to put the Potters on level terms, but it was no more than they deserved after some enterprising play. The teams went down the tunnel at half-time with the game delicately poised.

However, Liverpool took the fixture away from Stoke City with three goals in the first ten minutes of the second half. First of all, on 47 minutes, Roger Hunt headed home after winger Thompson cut inside his defender and crossed, followed two minutes later when Arrowsmith once more fed the dangerous Thompson and he again crossed for Hunt to steer a header past Stoke City keeper Leslie. Then, young Alf Arrowsmith netted on 53

Ian St John in action for Liverpool v Stoke City on Boxing Day 1963.

minutes, after Hunt had scampered down the left wing and pulled the ball back to him – game over.

As Stoke visibly tired, Liverpool poured forward and Hunt once again scored on 73 minutes when he slid Milne's pass under Leslie to complete his hat-trick and make it 5-1. Hunt then went one better on 81 minutes, slamming in Liverpool's sixth, and his fourth, after showing excellent control in a crowded area. Quite an achievement to score four in a single half in a First Division fixture.

This was the cue for the Kop – a swaying, standing terrace in those days – to burst into the Beatles song 'We Love You, Yeah,Yeah,Yeah', making it a wonderful Christmas for Koppites.

This result took Liverpool up to third with 32 points, two points behind Blackburn Rovers and just one behind Spurs. It set the Reds up nicely for a run to the title, which they achieved so effectively.

Roger Hunt.

In the weeks following, Liverpool also scored six versus Sheffield United and Ipswich Town, and memorably five against Arsenal on 18 April, to ultimately clinch the title. Seven straight wins and 21 goals scored, from 20 March up to the Arsenal fixture on 18 April, proved ultimately decisive.

Stoke City had fought well on Merseyside, especially in the first half, but their season would not be defined by this result. Their focus remained on survival, which they achieved by winning 14 fixtures, ending the season in 17th position with 38 points, ten clear of the relegation zone.

They were building for the future and succeeded in season 1963/64 with several more mid-table finishes, before winning the League Cup in 1972 with a team, remembered fondly in the Potteries, that included Ritchie, Conroy, Smith, Banks and Eastham. They also developed an exceptional side in the mid-70s, with players such as the gifted Alan Hudson, finishing fifth twice in consecutive seasons (1973/74 and 1974/75), and actually topping the table briefly in both seasons before being sadly relegated back to Division Two in 1976/77 after a 15-season run in the top flight.

Liverpool FC 1963/64.

Return Match

 Stoke City
3-1
Liverpool

Date: 29 April **Venue:** Victoria Ground **Att:** 32,149

The original return fixture scheduled for 28 December was postponed so the game was not held until late April, by which time Liverpool had been confirmed as champions despite only gaining one point from their last three fixtures – all away from Anfield.

In front of an excellent attendance of 32,149, Stoke City very graciously formed a guard of honour to welcome the Liverpool team onto the pitch. Liverpool resisted making wholesale changes and put out essentially their championship-winning team. Gerry Byrne at right-back and Chris Lawler at centre-half were the only two changes from the Boxing Day line-up. The Stoke team contained two changes – young John Flowers came in along with a change of goalkeeper, with Bobby Irvine replacing Lawrie Leslie.

With Liverpool already crowned champions and Stoke City safe, and the game being the last fixture of the season for both teams, you may have expected a fixture with a testimonial feel to it, but not a bit of it.

It was a highly watchable game, with intensity and a desire to win from both clubs. The *Liverpool Echo* noted that it was more like the first fixture of the season rather than the last in its intensity.

However, the guard of honour was the only concession the home club gave Liverpool all evening. From the kick-off it became clear this would be a competitive fixture and Stoke made the early running with McIlroy prominent and Viollet and Ritchie threatening the Liverpool defenders, but it was Liverpool who had the best chances.

After 20 minutes a wonderful header from St John was brilliantly saved by Irvine, then shortly afterwards Irvine could only parry a powerful shot by Thompson up in the air. Thankfully for Stoke, Arrowsmith was unable to score from the rebound, as Kennell cleared off the line with an overhead kick. As half-time approached both Ritchie and Viollet had presentable chances to score, but Liverpool custodian Lawrence saved both efforts, ensuring a 0-0 scoreline at half-time in a very watchable game.

The status-quo lasted just three minutes into the second half. A corner by Denis Viollet resulted in unusually slack Liverpool defending, allowing the unmarked Bebbington to finish well, past Lawrence who had no chance.

Liverpool levelled just after the hour mark when a quick throw-in beat Kinnell to find Arrowsmith and the youngster beat Irvine with a well-taken shot. Parity was to last just seven minutes, when a Viollet cross from the corner flag found McIlroy, who dummied the ball allowing John Ritchie to crash it home.

Shortly afterwards St John nearly equalised with a header that hit the inside of the post and came out.

Liverpool poured forward late on with Peter Thompson nearly scoring with a powerful drive. However, they were caught on the break shortly afterwards when Dobing finished off a move to make the game safe for Stoke City, to send their fans home happy. An excellent and well-deserved win for the Potters.

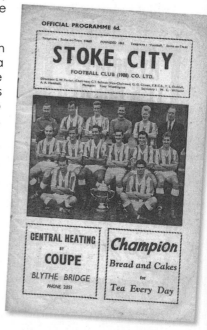

PLAYER PROFILE
Roger Hunt

Born in Culcheth, Bolton, on 20 July 1938, Roger Hunt was one of the best goalscorers of his generation and will forever be part of our English football fabric as one of the XI who won the World Cup for England that July afternoon in 1966.

His path to professional football, however, was not the normal one, as Roger had to work hard and wait for his chance.

He signed for Second Division Bury as a 17-year-old, as they were the only club to give him a trial after he had written to all the local professional clubs. The trial went well and Hunt was signed on amateur forms. He trained two nights a week, playing at the weekend, whilst still undertaking his duties at the haulage company that his father Richard owned. However, that schedule soon became too much of a commitment for the young player.

Hunt asked for a full-time contract, but all he was offered was a month. He only played twice in that period, as Bury already had a full staff roster. As a result, Hunt felt Bury were unsure about him and so he returned to the family business.

He continued to play, however, turning out for Stockton Heath Albion (now Warrington Town), then Devizes Town, whilst he was stationed in Wiltshire in the army. It was whilst playing for Stockton Heath (whilst on army leave) that he was spotted by Liverpool scout Bill Jones.

Hunt signed for the Reds aged 20, playing for the Central League team after being demobbed from the army. It was a real stroke of luck, but Roger had a real fight on his hands to establish himself at Anfield.

He need not have worried.

In his first five games for Liverpool reserves he scored seven times and the then Liverpool boss, Phil Taylor, soon picked him for the first team in a match against Scunthorpe in the Second Division in front of 32,000 under the lights at Anfield. Hunt seized his chance by scoring in the 64th minute to secure a 2-0 win for Liverpool – the first of 245 league goals, a club record that still stands today.

Bill Shankly replaced Phil Taylor in 1959, but Hunt survived the player clear-out that ensued, going on to become an integral player for both Liverpool and England throughout the 60s.

With Hunt as their regular scorer, Liverpool set about getting promotion to the First Division. From season 1958/59 they finished fourth, third and third again, before finally winning the Second Division in style in season 1961/62, losing just seven games, with Hunt having his best season yet, scoring 41 in 41 appearances.

Liverpool (and Hunt) felt at home in the top flight, finishing seventh and setting the foundations for the season to follow when they won the First

A rare image of Roger Hunt scoring on his debut on 9 September 1959.

Hunt scoring for Liverpool against Inter Milan at Anfield.

Division championship with three games to spare. They won 16 home fixtures, scoring a mammoth 92 goals, with Hunt in his pomp – another 31 goals.

The reward for winning the league was qualification for the European Cup the following season, with Liverpool easing to the semi-finals where they met Italian giants Inter Milan over two legs. The Reds won the first leg 3-1 under the lights at a throbbing Anfield, with a trademark goal from Hunt, but they lost the second leg 3-0 in very controversial circumstances at the San Siro, with what have been described at two 'highly debatable' goals.

In 1965 Hunt starred again, as Liverpool won the FA Cup followed by the league title in 1965/66, with the prolific Hunt bagging another 29 goals. Hunt was then involved in a highly unusual incident which was seemingly out of character for him. Liverpool were playing Leicester City in an FA Cup fifth-round replay at Anfield and were losing 1-0 when the Reds missed a penalty (saved by a young Peter Shilton). Liverpool manager Bill Shankly decided to substitute Hunt to try another option to break Leicester down. It is fair to say Hunt was unimpressed and ripped off his shirt, throwing it at the bench on the way to the changing rooms.

That incident, along with a little drop in form and the aging of the mid-60s team, signalled the end of the Hunt era at Liverpool and he left for Bolton Wanderers in December 1969, although Hunt felt that he could have stayed at Anfield a bit longer – he had just turned 31.

Hunt had two and a half seasons at Bolton in the Second and then Third Divisions, making 76 appearances, scoring 24 goals, before calling it a day in May 1972 aged almost 34. In all competitions Hunt scored 309 goals in 568 fixtures – not bad for a player who felt he would not make it after failing to establish himself at Bury.

His international career started when playing for Liverpool in the Second Division. His form alerted England boss Walter Winterbottom, who gave Hunt his first cap on 4 April 1962 in a friendly versus Austria and – typically – Hunt scored as England won 3-1. He travelled to Chile with England for the 1962 World Cup but did not take the field, but he continued to play for England between World Cups. When the squad was announced for the 1966 tournament, Hunt was initially miffed to be given the number 21 shirt, but he need not have worried as he played all six fixtures, scoring three times, helping England to win the World Cup. In all, Hunt scored 18 times for England in 34 appearances and his unselfish play was respected by all of his 1966 team-mates.

Club rules meant that player testimonials were granted only after the player had finished playing, so Hunt had to wait until he had left Bolton to qualify for his. The wait was worth it, however, as on a memorable night at Anfield (11 April 1972), under torrential rain, the entire Liverpool 1965 FA Cup-winning XI played an England XI that included most of the 1966 World Cup-winning team.

It was indicative of the love all connected with Liverpool FC had for Hunt, that Anfield was full an hour before kick-off, with thousands locked outside. The attendance of 56,000 saw Liverpool win 8-6, with a hat-

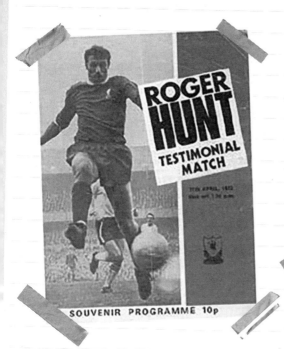

trick from Hunt who still looked as if he could play, such was the ease with which he moved around the pitch. It was a memorable evening despite the rain, raising £24,000 – a big sum in 1972!

Hunt was honoured by his 'knighthood' – not in the conventional sense but from the Kop who would forever call him Sir Roger Hunt.

After his playing career was over, Hunt initially worked in the family haulage business. He was also a member of the Pools Panel before retiring and playing plenty of golf. He received a somewhat belated MBE in 2000 and was inducted into the English Football Hall of Fame in 2006. Only Ian Rush has scored more goals for Liverpool in competitive fixtures, but Roger retains the record for League goals with 245.

As I write, Hunt is alive and well, aged 79 and living in Warrington.

John Henry Ritchie

Born 12 July 1941 in Kettering, Northamptonshire, Ritchie was the subject of a very bizarre signing but turned out to be one of the finest players in the history of Stoke City FC. To this day, he is their record goalscorer, and is much loved and much missed.

Stoke City's canny manager Tony Waddington was having a casual conversation with his friend Arthur Turner (ex-Stoke City from the 1930s) who had transformed Headington United into Oxford United. Arthur just happened to mention to Tony that the Oxford United board would not release £2,500 to sign a non-league goalscorer who had scored 40 goals in two seasons for Kettering Town. That player, of course, was John Ritchie, who was playing for his home-town club whilst working full-time in the shoe industry in the town.

Ritchie had come to notice when Kettering beat Third Division Swindon Town (including Mike Summerbee and Ernie Hunt) 3-0 in the FA Cup first-round replay in 1961, in front of over 8,000, after coming back from 2-0 down in Wiltshire to draw 2-2. Ritchie, as a 20-year-old, scored in the replay and caused professional defenders – who were playing three divisions higher – problems all night with his power and physical presence.

Kettering Town were a leading non-league club at the time, with good facilities, and had won the Southern League championship with Ritchie's help in 1961. Sniffing a bargain, Tony Waddington phoned around some of his extensive contacts that afternoon and received favourable feedback about Ritchie and persuaded the Stoke City board to take a punt on him at £2,500. And as it turned out, it was one of, if not the best buy in the history of The Potters.

Ritchie at Stoke City.

Tony called Kettering Town with the offer, forcing their club secretary to cycle to Ritchie's work place in Kettering to tell him the news. Ritchie did not immediately recognise the manager's name, as Stoke were a Second Division side back then, but he called Stoke back anyway ... and the rest is history!

It was the first and only time that Tony Waddington bought a player without ever seeing him play. Stoke initially offered Ritchie a one-year deal but he argued that two years would be fairer, allowing him time to settle as a full-time professional player. Waddington eventually agreed and Ritchie signed for Stoke in 1962.

The next day, Turner called Waddington back to say that he had finally agreed the £2,500 from the Oxford United board, as more locally Northampton Town had also been sniffing round Ritchie. An interesting conversation no doubt ensued, although it is not documented whether Waddington's opportunism compromised their friendship, but his nimbleness certainly benefitted Stoke City for a decade.

It is reported that Ritchie's wife Shirley 'cried all the way from Kettering to the Potteries' for fear of getting homesick, but they settled well in the area, with the warmth of the locals being key.

The difference between training twice a week with Kettering to being a full-time athlete is a big one, and Ritchie took some time to settle. He also had to cope with a drop in total pay, as his initial Stoke City wages were not as good as his combined income from working and being a part-time non-league player.

He made his first-team debut in Stoke's promotion season of 1962/63, but it wasn't until the following season that he enjoyed a decent run in the team. He was called into the side as they looked to establish themselves back in the First Division and his strength, aerial ability and a surprising amount of skill, for such a big guy, soon shone through. He began to score regularly, eventually notching 18 goals in 29 games, including goals in both fixtures versus champions Liverpool, as we have seen – a great effort for someone who had been a non-league player just two years previously.

After being a regular in the side for over four seasons, he was surprisingly sold to Sheffield Wednesday for £80,000 in the 1966/67 season as manager Waddington felt he had lost his effectiveness. The *Stoke Sentinel* reports that hundreds of letters poured into their office expressing surprise at the transfer and questioning – politely – the sanity of the Stoke board in letting Ritchie go – the 1966 version of a social media campaign!

Sheffield Wednesday were so keen to sign Ritchie that they allowed him to continue to live in the Potteries. He spent three years in Yorkshire and had a decent record there too, scoring 45 goals in 106 appearances in all competitions. However, in his third season (1968/69) he struggled somewhat and did not fit into manager Danny Williams's plans.

Tony Waddington admitted his initial mistake in letting Ritchie go by re-signing him for £28,000 – much to the relief of all in the Potteries – and the problem of how to replace John Ritchie was resolved!

Ritchie was actually on holiday in Bournemouth with his family when the hotel manager called him in from the pool when Waddington phoned, with the words that would change his life: 'It's Tony Waddington – I think he wants to re-sign you.' Ritchie said yes on the spot and was brought back home to the Potteries, thus becoming Stoke's best signing – twice!

Waddington's idea was to partner Ritchie with Jimmy Greenhoff and it worked a treat, as Ritchie top scored in three of the next four seasons, helping the side to two FA Cup semi-finals, losing both to Arsenal. Stoke were very unlucky in both games.

However, Stoke secured their first-ever trophy by winning the League Cup at Wembley in season 1971/72, with Ritchie being an integral part of the success. He scored regularly in the 11 fixtures that it took to win the trophy. Readers of a certain vintage may recall a wonderful penalty save by Gordon Banks in the semi-final second leg at Upton Park, which Gordon rated alongside his famous save from Pele as his two best ever saves – thankfully the footage survives on YouTube.

One of Ritchie's qualities that endeared him to the Stoke City fans was that he took no nonsense from anybody, even if that meant occasionally paying the consequences.

A benefit of Stoke winning the League Cup was UEFA Cup European football in 1972/73. Stoke were drawn against the German outfit Kaiserslautern, winning the home leg 3-1, with Ritchie scoring late on. However, in the away leg Stoke were 3-0 down, and, with Ritchie on the bench, he was called on to try and salvage something. But as he entered the field one of the German players (Hosic) punched him in the kidneys and Ritchie retaliated. Sadly referee Eksztajn only saw the retaliation - and the prone Hosic – and so dismissed Ritchie after 29 seconds without him going anywhere near the football. Stoke lost 4-0 and crashed out of Europe.

Very sadly for Ritchie (and for Stoke) he suffered a double leg break in a tangle with Kevin Beattie of Ipswich Town in September 1974 which effectively ended his career at 33. This caused a little bad blood between the teams and in the return fixture Stoke City's Denis Smith was involved in an incident with Allan Hunter, who also broke his leg.

After recovering from this terrible injury, Ritchie did try a comeback with local non-league club Stafford Rangers, but to no avail, and his career as a professional footballer was done.

He stayed local and ran a pottery business with his wife until he sadly passed away on 23 February 2007 aged just 65, after a long battle with Alzheimer's Disease.

Ritchie's record of 176 Stoke City goals in 347 appearances in all competitions is an impressive one and he is still their record goalscorer. Commanding an original transfer fee of £2,500, that means each goal cost £14.20 – a decent return for a punt of a transfer.

Ritchie at Wembley – one of the highlights of his career.

John's funeral was held on 7 March 2007 at Stoke Minster and caused big traffic problems as seemingly most of the Potteries wanted to say farewell to 'Big John' – one of the most wholehearted and committed footballers to ever wear the famous red and white stripes and a footballer whom the Potteries had adopted as one of their own. In modern football banter and parlance, the question is often asked, 'Could the player do it on a wet Tuesday night in Stoke?' Well John Ritchie could – and then some.

The last word on John Ritchie accompanies his bust outside the Boothen End at the Stoke City stadium – an honour that's reserved for those very few footballers who made an indelible mark on a football club and on a community. It reads:

'Lives on in our hearts as one of Staffordshire's greatest sporting heroes'

Rest In Peace.

SCOREBOARD

	RED INDICATOR	H.T.	Final		WHITE INDICATOR	H.T.	Final
A	Boton Wanderers .... Sheffield Wednesday			**A**	Plymouth Argyle .... Southampton		
B	Aston Villa .... Wolverhampton Wanderers			**B**	Portsmouth .... Bury		
C	Birmingham City .... Arsenal			**C**	Preston North End .... Cardiff City		
D	Blackburn Rovers .... West Ham United			**D**	Rotherham United .... Northampton Town		
E	Chelsea .... Blackpool			**E**	Scunthorpe United .... Manchester City		
F	Everton .... Leicester City			**F**	Sunderland .... Leeds United		
G	Ipswich Town .... Fulham			**G**	Swindon Town .... Norwich City		
H	Manchester United .... Burnley			**H**	Coventry City .... Barnsley		
I	Stoke City .... Liverpool			**I**	Mansfield Town .... Hull City		
J	Tottenham Hotspur .... West Bromwich Albion			**J**	Bradford .... Lincoln City		
K	Charlton Athletic .... Swansea Town			**K**	Darlington .... York City		
L	Derby County .... Middlesbrough			**L**	Doncaster Rovers .... Southport		
M	Huddersfield Town .... Newcastle United			**M**	Gillingham .... Chesterfield		
N	Leyton Orient .... Grimsby Town			**N**	Bury Reserves .... Sheffield United Reserves ..		

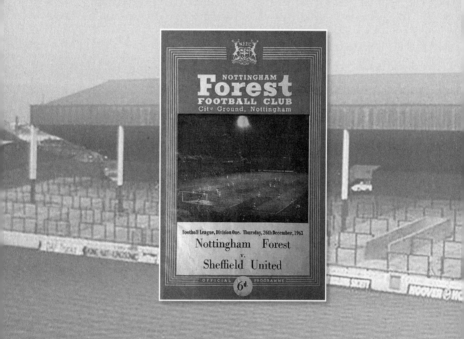

Chapter 8

Nottingham Forest v Sheffield United

3 - 3

Kick-off: 3pm   **Venue: City Ground**   **Attendance: 23,800**

Grummitt	1	Thompson
Grant	2	Coldwell
Mochan	3	B. Shaw
Newton	4	Richardson
McKinlay	5	J. Shaw
Whitefoot	6	Summers
Kear	7	Allchurch ⚽
Quigley	8	Ash
⚽ Wignall	9	Jones ⚽⚽
⚽ Vowden	10	Wagstaff
⚽ Storey-Moore	11	Hartle

The Managers

Johnny Carey   John Harris

Match Report

After seven goals at Anfield, we return to the East Midlands for a game between two closely matched teams that would go on to finish mid-table in 12th and 13th position at the end of the season.

It was very muddy on the banks of the River Trent, resulting in a heavy pitch, but the two teams served up another treat for fans with a blistering start, a spirited fightback, a penalty, a last-minute equaliser, an almost-even later winner, a mini-pitch invasion and six goals.

Nottingham Forest, at this point, were still 15 years away from their First Division title triumph of 1978 following promotion from Division Two the previous season. In the 1960s they were very much a middling club, finishing ninth in 1962/63, but flirting with relegation in two of the previous three seasons. They had in their ranks the emerging talent of Ian Storey-Moore – an attacking player at just 18 years old who had been picked up from Scunthorpe. Forest were managed by Johnny Carey, who also managed the Republic of Ireland in his spare time.

Forest started the 1963/64 season in great style, winning 2-1 in their first away fixture at eventual champions Liverpool, showing the potential of the group, and were involved in some high-scoring away fixtures – losing 4-2 at Arsenal, 3-1 at Sheffield Wednesday and drawing 3-3 at Birmingham. Their form at home in the autumn was generally good, with comfortable wins over Wolves, West Ham, Bolton, Ipswich and Leicester, although they had been beaten the previous week at home versus Spurs.

However, Forest came into the Boxing Day fixture without a win in seven games and sat in 13th position. They were a solid team – neither able to compete for the top eight or be threatened with the bottom six and thoughts of relegation.

Ian Storey-Moore

Nottingham Forest in 1963/64.

Sheffield United were actually top after 15 fixtures of the 1963/64 season – beating eventual champions Liverpool 3-0 along the way – and had some talented footballers on their books at that time. Memorable away wins at Stoke, West Ham, Aston Villa, Burnley and Leicester helped keep them in the upper reaches of the table and they had a defensive structure that had served them well in away fixtures.

United were managed by 'Gentleman' John Harris but had faded a bit as autumn turned to winter and went into this fixture on Trentside in eighth position, albeit that was five positions above their opponents that Boxing Day. They were on a run of only one win in six and needed to regain the form they showed earlier in the season if they wanted to climb the table.

On a very heavy pitch, Forest – in their famous Garibaldi red shirts with white shorts – were all over the Blades in the first half, coming out of the traps to run United ragged, with Storey-Moore and Kear especially prominent down the flanks. They won a succession of early corners and opened the scoring when ex-Evertonian Frank Wignall headed home from one such corner. The lead was doubled after only 13 minutes when Geoff Vowden scored from a rebound after Blades goalkeeper Des Thompson spilled a shot.

Forest completed the ferocious opening burst with a top-class third goal on 17 minutes when the talented Ian Storey-Moore scored with a right-footed shot into the top corner that gave Thompson no chance. 3-0 up after just over a quarter of an hour and the game was almost won already. It was so nearly 4-0 when Vowden saw a shot wonderfully saved by Thompson in the Sheffield United goal – perhaps a defining moment in this football match.

Sheffield United in 1963/64.

It is reported that United did get a modicum of control as half-time approached, but nobody foresaw what happened after the break.

The *Sheffield Telegraph*, with a nice turn of phrase, described the performance as 'Like Babes in the Pantomine Wood – lost, ragged and despondent.' Could manager John Harris inspire his troops to get back into the game for the second half? When asked after the fixture what he said at the break, Harris said, 'I just told them to compete more for the ball as opposed to letting it come to you.' And that simple instruction seemed to work, as Sheffield United escaped back 35 miles north with a point that did not look likely for much of the first half.

The Blades were sharper to the ball in the second half, and on the hour mark young Mick Jones volleyed the ball home following a cross from the right to reduce the arrears to two. Just five minutes later Barry Hartle – whose speed from the left wing had caused Forest some problems – was upended in the box, and Len Allchurch scored with ease from the spot to bring United back into the fixture with 25 minutes still to play.

Despite United now pushing forward, it looked like Forest would hang on for a narrow victory, but with the last few seconds ticking away Michael Ash cleverly beat Forest centre-half Bob McKinley with a pass that sent Jones clear of the defence. The young centre-forward showed maturity way beyond his years to beat the on-rushing Grummitt with a left-foot shot into the corner to salvage a point for Sheffield United. There were, however, still a few seconds left and the Blades almost scored a fourth when Jones had a half chance, but Forest were relieved to clear their lines.

As the final whistle blew the travelling away fans – who must have feared the worst at half time – broke through the flimsy stewarding to cheer their heroes off the pitch, and it must have felt like a win to them. Sheffield United had continued their impressive away form but they left it late, and that fine save by Thompson, to prevent it becoming 4-0, was indeed decisive.

Return Match

Sheffield United
1-2
Nottingham Forest

Date: 28 December   **Venue:** Bramall Lane   **Att:** 24,865

Forest made the short trip to Bramall Lane 48 hours later, which in those days was a three-sided stadium as it was still a venue for first-class cricket. The fact there was nothing between the sides was once again demonstrated with another close game.

Forest won the return fixture 2-1 and Ian Storey-Moore once again took the eye with two goals for Forest, whilst Michael Ash replied for the Blades in front of 24,865.

First-class cricket being played at Bramall Lane, Sheffield, in 1961.

Following their win at Bramall Lane, Forest would win their next two away fixtures at Wolves and Blackburn, and despite shipping six at Goodison Park (in Fred Pickering's first fixture for Everton) they finished the season in mid-table.

Nottingham Forest would go on to finish fifth the following season, inspired by Storey-Moore, but slumped to 17th before bizarrely mounting a title challenge in season 1966/67, finishing second to Manchester United. However, that was as good as it got for that group of players, who then faded back into mid-table before getting relegated in 1971/72.

After a few seasons of being a lower, mid-table club in the Second Division, their destiny was to change when the genius Brian Clough joined them in 1975, and the rest is well-documented history.

Sheffield United performed solidly after the Christmas period, finishing the season in 12th, but the following year they finished in the bottom four, before rising to eighth in 1965/66 and tenth in 1966/67. However, they were sadly relegated the following season before returning to the top flight in the early 70s with a well-recalled team including Alan Woodward and Tony Currie.

Brian Clough joins Nottingham Forest in 1975 – precursor to a golden period in Forest's rich history.

PLAYER PROFILE
Michael David Jones

Born in Shireoaks near Worksop, Nottinghamshire, on 24 April 1945, Jones had a decent start on his football journey that was ultimately so sadly cut short by injury.

His father was goalkeeper for Worksop Town, a senior non-league club south-east of Sheffield, near to where Jones was born. He was a regular visitor to both Bramall Lane and Hillsborough as an enthusiastic, football-loving youth.

Mick Jones – Sheffield United.

Jones was an outstanding young footballer and once scored 14 goals in a school fixture. He was unsurprisingly spotted by Sheffield United when he was playing for Dinnington Miners' Welfare and joined them as an apprentice as a 16-year-old in 1961. He developed very quickly through the junior and reserve-team ranks with considerable success, before making his Blades debut in April 1963 versus Manchester United in a 1-1 draw at Old Trafford, aged just 17. Four days later, on his 18th birthday, he scored his first two goals as centre-forward in a 3-1 win against Manchester City at Maine Road and his Bramall Lane career was up and running.

Jones continued to lead the line, in season 1963/64, with distinction for such a young man, and he garnered ten appearances for England U23s (some after he had made his full England debut) and his progress was such that he made two appearances for England in 1965. His international debut was in May 1965 versus West Germany in Munich (England won 1-0 with a goal from Terry Paine), followed by another cap four days later versus Sweden in Gothenburg on the same tour (England won 2-1 with goals from Alan Ball and John Connelly). These caps were won just 18 and 22 days after his 20th birthday, and six members of the England side that played 12 months later to win the World Cup played that evening. Jones was a traditional centre-forward – 5ft 11in tall and weighing 11st 10lbs. He was strong, good in the air but also had two good feet. He had an impressive goal record allied to an admirable work ethic and gave experienced defenders plenty of problems, but sadly for him he was not selected for the England squad for the 1966 World Cup.

He was a regular for the Blades for four full seasons, starting in 1963/64, and 21 goals in the 1965/66 season was a very decent effort. He also formed a very good partnership with Alan Birchenall.

This level of success was inevitably going to attract envious glances from other clubs and there was considerable upset and angst within the Bramall Lane faithful when Sheffield United manager John Harris accepted a bid of £100,000 for his services from Yorkshire neighbours Leeds United in November 1967. It has to be noted that Leeds manager Don Revie was very careful with his club's funds and this was the first time Leeds had signed a player for a fee of that magnitude, but at his age and with his record it was considered a valid gamble. Jones was still only 22 but had scored a highly respectable 72 goals in 176 appearances in all competitions for Sheffield United, and he was an experienced First Division footballer at an age when he could still develop further.

As an added bonus for Jones he did not have to move house. Harris would later remark, 'It would be the biggest mistake the club ever made.'

Jones was a very canny signing for Leeds United as they had settled back into the First Division after promotion in 1963/64. They were developing a team under Don Revie who would compete strongly for both domestic and European honours for a decade, and Jones was an integral part of that talented and combative group.

His initial brief from his manager Don Revie was to 'score goals and be a pest to defenders' – a brief carried out to perfection for over seven seasons and over 300 fixtures in all competitions.

Jones's third, and final, England cap was in January 1970 (five years after his first) when he played in a 0-0 draw at Wembley versus the Netherlands. He was named as an official reserve for the 1970 World Cup in Mexico and had all the necessary inoculations and medical certificates needed

to go, but in the event he was not required and his international career was over. Some, to this day, feel that was a criminal return of caps for such a talented player, even allowing for the riches of attacking talent England had during that period.

Jones with a dislocated shoulder in the 1972 FA Cup Final. Despite his injury, he insisted on climbing the steps to collect his medal. He assisted greatly in the winning goal scored by Allan Clarke.

Allan Clarke (left) and Mick Jones celebrating a goal for Leeds versus Manchester United in February 1972. They formed a great partnership.
This was the first in a 15-minute hat-trick in a 5-1 win.

During Jones's time at Leeds he was much decorated with trophies – two league titles, leading scorer in 1968/69 (without Allan Clarke) and in 1973/74, three times a runner-up, FA Cup winner in 1972 (when he injured himself) and twice a runner-up including 1970 when he scored in both the finals versus Chelsea (at Wembley in a 2-2 draw and in the very physical replay at Old Trafford, which Leeds lost 2-1). He also won the League Cup in 1968 and was twice a winner in Europe – the full set – all three domestic trophies plus one in Europe. Not too shabby.

Leeds were a superb side in that era, showing a unity as a band of brothers – and many argue their trophy haul did not reflect their ability – albeit they were not universally loved as they had a reputation for a physical approach, and whilst they could look after themselves they could play and regularly destroyed teams with their passing and movement.

Very sadly, whilst at Leeds, Jones suffered a career-ending injury in 1975, aged just 30, having scored 111 goals in 309 Leeds appearances. He was integral to that Leeds United team of the late 1960s and early 1970s, and was the ideal foil to Allan Clarke. In fact, Jones scored double figures in each of his seven seasons as a regular in that renowned Leeds United side and top-scored both times that the Revie side won the First Division.

Allan Clarke is on record as saying that he was never the same player after Jones's retirement and it has been frequently suggested that Jones was the bludgeon to Clarke's rapier, but he was better than that – much better.

Jones was the sort of player that all clubs need – talented in his own right, honest, reliable and prepared to do all the running to create opportunities for colleagues. He was a players' player and would often be regarded as an unsung hero. He was in that Elland Road changing room for seven years – a room full of big personalities – but he never felt the need for adulation, which, arguably, some of the others felt more comfortable with.

In all competitions, Jones played in 485 fixtures with two great Yorkshire clubs and scored 187 goals in the top flight and various cup competitions, even though he never played after his 30th birthday.

After his playing days were cut so short, Jones became a representative for sportswear company Sondico and then ran a successful sports shop in Maltby, near Doncaster, for 14 years until 2000, ran a market stall selling sportswear with his son, and, like many of the surviving members of that iconic Leeds United team of the late 60s and early 70s, he was employed to host hospitality at Elland Road on matchdays.

OFFICIAL PROGRAMME
PRICE SIXPENCE

SHEFFIELD WEDNESDAY
LEAGUE DIVISION ONE FOOTBALL
Hillsborough

SHEFFIELD WEDNESDAY
versus
BOLTON WANDERERS
ON THURSDAY, 26th DECEMBER, 1963
KICK-OFF 3.0 P.M.

Chapter 9

Sheffield Wednesday v Bolton Wanderers
3 - 0

Kick-off: 3pm   Venue: Hillsborough   Attendance: 32,301

MacLaren	1	Hopkinson
B. Hill	2	Hartle
Megson	3	Farrimond
McAnearney	4	Hatton
Swan	5	Hulme
Young	6	Lennard
Wilkinson	7	Davison
⚽⚽ Dobson	8	Lee
Layne	9	Davies
⚽ Pearson	10	Deakin
Halliday	11	F. Hill

The Managers
Vic Buckingham   Bill Ridding

Match Report

Sheffield Wednesday were a top-six club in the late 1950s and early 1960s – a consistent spell of competing for trophies for the Owls second only to their success in the 1930s when they won back-to-back league titles and competed with the great Arsenal side of that period. Their Second Division promotion side of 1959 was under Harry Catterick and the side instantly made an impression back at the highest level – finishing fifth and reaching the FA Cup semi-final, where they lost unluckily to Blackburn Rovers.

The following season (1960/61) they were unlucky to cross swords with the outstanding Spurs double-winning team – Wednesday only lost seven fixtures that season and their points total as runners-up would have made them champions the season before – and the season after! It was also the season that included one of the most memorable Wednesday victories of all time – a 7-2 win at Old Trafford in an FA Cup fourth-round replay on 1 February 1961 with goals from Ellis (3), Fantham (2) and Finney (2). This was indeed a talented Wednesday outfit.

Sadly for Wednesday, Catterick decamped for Everton towards the end of the 1960/61 season, to be replaced by Vic Buckingham, but their consistency continued and Sheffield Wednesday were a top-six side for five seasons – after promotion in 1959, they finished fifth, second, sixth, sixth and sixth again in 1963/64.

Sheffield Wednesday in 1963/64. Note Peter Swan – back row, far right – who would show off his extraordinary physique by wearing his shorts high!

In season 1963/64 the goals flowed immediately with a 3-3 draw versus Manchester United in their first game. They also scored three in successive home fixtures versus Fulham and Ipswich Town, and won 4-1 in Utrecht in an Inter Cities Fairs Cup first-leg tie – a reward for their league position the previous season. They also won the home leg 4-1 and progressed through but sadly were beaten by Cologne in both legs in the next round. Wednesday's league form continued to be good and they went into the Christmas period in fifth position and in good form – particularly at home where they beat Forest 3-1 and Wolves 5-0 and had a memorable 4-4 draw at Stoke City – goals aplenty for Owls fans.

In the Wednesday line-up that Boxing Day were some notable footballers: Don Megson, whose son Gary also played for Wednesday, Colin Dobson, a clever forward, and Peter Swan and David 'Bronco' Layne who would attract a different sort of notoriety in 1964.

Bolton Wanderers at that period were enjoying a run of 30 consecutive seasons in the First Division, from 1934, and had competed for the major honours for some of that time. They had won the FA Cup in 1958, beating Manchester United 2-0 at Wembley with two goals from their talisman and most famous player Nat Lofthouse. This 30-year spell is regarded as a 'golden period' by Trotters fans of a certain vintage, although the 1958 FA Cup would be the last major trophy the club would win to the present day.

That cup-final victory deprived the Red Devils of a very emotional cup win as the Munich disaster had happened just three months earlier and United got through to the final with a patched-up team and considerable public sentiment. Bolton were on a high in the late 1950s and finished fourth and sixth in the two seasons following, but thereafter a decline set in resulting in bottom-five finishes in two out of the next three seasons. As a result, they approached the 1963/64 season with a degree of apprehension.

They were right to do that as the writing was on the wall early – Bolton lost their first five fixtures, with their first victory coming in their seventh game when they put six past Ipswich Town in mid-September. Once again there were plenty of goals about as Bolton lost 4-3 at Arsenal and 4-3 at home to Stoke City.

Coming into the Boxing Day fixture at Hillsborough, Bolton had only won three times in the league and were already looking like a relegation outfit – only the ineptness of Ipswich was keeping Wanderers off the bottom.

There were, however, some footballers of note in the Bolton line-up that day – young Francis Lee would go on to be a Manchester City legend as a player and owner, whilst Wyn Davies was a powerful centre-forward who served several clubs with distinction, including Newcastle United.

For the clash of these two grand old clubs, the *Sheffield Telegraph* reported that the Wednesday general manager Eric Taylor put out a pre-fixture message saying that pitch conditions were extremely difficult, with ice on the pitch, and to 'bear with the entertainers'.

In the initial stages of the game, both sets of players slid all over the place as 31,301 watched on at Hillsborough – one of the most impressive football theatres in England in the early 60s, as the visionary cantilever stand had been built for the 1966 World Cup.

Wednesday were without their usual goalkeeper Ron Springett, who was injured, to be replaced by Roy MacLaren. It took the players a while to get used to the conditions, but once the game settled down Wednesday,

The wonderful new stand at Hillsborough, built in time for the 1966 World Cup. At the time, it was a visionary cantilever design (no pillars!).

and England centre-half Peter Swan in particular, began to dominate. The Owls took the lead on 15 minutes when Colin Dobson found space and delicately chipped Bolton goalkeeper Eddie Hopkinson – Dobson was a highly skilful footballer and seemed to be one of the few players on the field unaffected by the conditions.

Wednesday were playing long and direct to account for the conditions with wing-halves McAnearney and Young playing particularly well, and they doubled their lead after 27 minutes when Pearson scored with another chip shot after being released by a through ball from Holliday. They went into half-time with a comfortable 2-0 lead, with Bolton struggling to come to terms with the conditions.

Despite a fair amount of possession, it took Bolton 63 minutes before they registered a shot on target, but Francis Lee's shot was straight at MacLaren. Bolton then lost their goalkeeper Hopkinson for 11 minutes after a clash with Peter Swan, Farrimond temporarily replacing him whilst he was treated (pre-substitute days), and for a while Bolton raised their game and showed a bit more bite in the tackle, but the outcome of the fixture was taken away from them on 80 minutes when Colin Dobson deflected a cross from Layne past Hopkinson for Wednesday's third goal.

Lennard did force a good save from MacLaren with a surging run through the middle, but it was Wednesday's afternoon and they held out comfortably enough to win 3-0 – a win that took Sheffield Wednesday to fourth in the First Division table.

The *Sheffield Telegraph* reported that the Owls' much more direct style of play was better suited to the conditions – very icy and wet – and the win was well deserved, although Bolton had their moments. However, this result still left Bolton Wanderers in big trouble in the bottom two with their 30-year occupancy of the First Division in serious doubt.

Return Match

 **Bolton Wanderers
3-0
Sheffield Wednesday**

Date: 28 December   **Venue:** Burnden Park   **Att:** 12,000

Pitch conditions were no better 48 hours later at Burnden Park, with the *Sheffield Telegraph* describing the playing surface as 'an absolute mud-heap'. Bolton made just one change in front of only 12,000 fans, who were not happy with the fare served up in an insipid first half. Neither team could generate any rhythm on the tricky surface. The only real chance came for Wednesday after 34 minutes when Pearson pulled the ball back from the byline, only for Dobson to chip over the gaping goal.

Many frustrated Bolton fans made their displeasure known to the players as they left the field for half-time with the score at 0-0. The Bolton manager is reported to have let his players have some of his wrath during the interval, pointing out that relegation was a distinct possibility unless they started to compete better in this sort of fixture.

The second half was better – it could hardly have been worse – and Wednesday should have been ahead, but it was Bolton who scored first on 57 minutes when Deakin rolled a free-kick to Lee, who blasted the ball between MacLaren and the defensive wall to wake up the fixture. On 60 minutes Deakin swept past Swan and Young and slammed the second past MacLaren. Wednesday couldn't recover and conceded again on 74 minutes when Wyn Davies scored from a rebound, after MacLaren failed to hold another shot from Deakin. Game over and a win for Bolton Wanderers, only their fourth in what was turning out to be a depressing season for the Trotters.

Wednesday went on to finish sixth that season and were mid-table at worst for several seasons after. They went to Wembley for the 1966 cup final, which they lost to Everton after being 2-0 ahead – a major disappointment. More disappointment soon followed, when, with the same ageing group of players, Wednesday were relegated in 1970 to the Second Division. Sadly for Wednesday, that was not the end of the decline and they were beset by financial issues and went down again in 1975 with just five wins in the Second Division. The following season they needed points from their last fixtures to avoid another drop but stayed up and began the long climb back to the First Division, achieved in 1984 under Howard Wilkinson after a successful spell by Jack Charlton.

In April 1964, just months after the Boxing Day fixture, Sheffield Wednesday were rocked by the '1964 Bribes Scandal' when three of their players were implicated in a betting fraud – taking money to ensure Wednesday lost in a 1962 fixture away at Ipswich – which they did 2-0. The players, Layne and Swan from the Boxing Day line-up and Tom Kay who had just signed for Everton, were jailed for four months and banned for life from the sport after being found guilty of defrauding bookmakers, but the ban was lifted in 1972.

Despite the welcome victory on 28 December, Bolton continued to struggle for the rest of the season but rallied a little in early April with three straight victories, including a 3-2 win at West Ham, which gave them some hope of survival as Birmingham continued to lose points. However, Bolton lost their last two fixtures versus Spurs and Wolves (0-4 at home) to go down one point shy of Birmingham, ending the 30-year streak and beginning a 25-year roller coaster, including nine changes of division.

As often happens, drops in momentum and belief are tough to arrest and Bolton were unable to come straight back up. In fact, they were relegated to the Third Division in 1971, although they came back to the Second Division in 1973 with an excellent side, including the imperious Frank Worthington. They climbed back to the top flight in 1978 ... only to be in the Fourth Division by 1987!

Thankfully, they enjoyed some good times in the Premier League after promotion in 2001 but are now back in the third tier, having seemingly overcome some severe financial difficulties, and it looks likely the journey back will have to begin in the fourth tier. History tells you, however, that Bolton Wanderers will be back at the highest level soon.

Peter Henry Swan

Born on 8 October 1936 in South Elmsall, Yorkshire, Peter Swan was an outstanding footballer – a ball-playing centre-half, lithe, athletic and a wonderful header of a football with an impressive physique – 6ft and 12 stone. He was one of the best defenders of his generation, who was a regular for England for over two years, playing 19 successive England fixtures after his debut in 1960, and he could have gone on to be one of England's all-time greats.

He was an integral member of the outstanding Sheffield Wednesday team that, from 1958 to 1964, was a top-six team, coming second in 1960/61. His fall from grace was a personal tragedy that we will look at shortly – it has been well documented elsewhere should you wish to delve deeper.

Swan was born into a large family of seven boys in the mining community of South Elmsall in West Yorkshire but moved to Doncaster and was initially a right-winger in schools football before being moved back to the defensive ranks when his physique developed. He was spotted by Sheffield Wednesday playing for Doncaster Schools and joined the Owls as an amateur in 1952, aged just 15, whilst working part-time in Armthorpe Colliery.

He signed as a part-time professional in 1953 and subsequently as a full-time pro in 1954, upon his 18th birthday, but was then called up for National Service, serving in the Royal Signals in Catterick, North Yorkshire, but they released him to play fixtures. His progress and talent was such that he made his debut on Bonfire Night 1955 versus Barnsley aged 19 but did not play regularly for over two seasons, finally becoming a regular early in the 1958/59 season as Wednesday began to have a very successful spell in the late 1950s and early 1960s – missing out only to Spurs for the title in 1960/61.

Swan's form was such that England honours were not far away and he made his debut aged 23 against Yugoslavia on 11 May 1960, and he played the next 19 fixtures leading up to the World Cup in Chile in 1962.

He was selected for the 1962 World Cup in Chile, but just before leaving he contracted tonsillitis, although he did recover and travel with the party, but whilst in South America he fell ill again with dysentery and did not play in the tournament, manager Winterbottom selecting the developing talent of Bobby Moore and the dependable Maurice Norman as centre-halves instead.

Swan would never play for England again, although Alf Ramsey let it be known that he was on the verge of being recalled in 1964 and was in mind for the 1966 World Cup squad, but then at the height of his career Swan became involved in one of the most defining football scandals of all time.

Peter Swan in action for England versus Scotland at Hampden Park in 1962, which England lost 2-0.

His indiscretion was getting involved with (although never meeting) Jimmy Gauld – a lower-league professional footballer and a goalscorer of some repute. Gauld had become 'The Fixer' for a gambling syndicate to bet on certain games knowing that some of the participants were 'on the inside'. Gauld had been a team-mate of David Layne at Swindon and the pair met up at Mansfield to watch a fixture. Gauld suggested to Layne that he could earn 'easy money' by throwing a fixture – betting on the outcome and sharing the proceeds.

Layne recruited Swan and Tony Kay – a Wednesday player at the time and another outstanding footballer who was later transferred to Everton for £60,000 and who had played for Everton as they won the title in 1962/63.

The First Division was an expansion for Gauld, whose activity to that point was in the lower leagues, and the three Wednesday players selected to play at Ipswich in December 1962 bet £50 each (just under two weeks' wages) on odds of 2-1 for them to lose.

Ray Crawford scored early for Ipswich, after the ball rebounded from the post, and Ipswich won fair and square. In fact, Kay got Man of the Match and it is reported that Swan played in his usual assured fashion.

The match that was to change Swan's life forever.

Swan later described in his book that he wasn't sure what he would have done had the fixture been level in the closing stages. The pay-out was £150 per man – about five weeks' wages – and it is estimated that the bookmakers lost £35,000 that week.

The scandal was exposed when 'The Fixer' Gauld was caught by the *Sunday People* – a ferocious investigative newspaper in its day – fixing some lower-league fixtures. Thereafter, Gauld effectively worked for the *People* (for a fee of £7,000 – over £130,000 today) by setting up those involved by discussing their bets in a car rigged with microphones. It would eventually become the first time taped evidence was used in a UK Court of Law.

The newspaper, as ever, wanted the 'big fish' – First Division and international footballers – and eventually the trail captured Swan, Layne and Kay, with the story breaking in April 1964 to widespread disbelief. The two remaining Wednesday players were removed by the FA from a fixture versus Spurs in April 1964, having been named in the programme and been getting ready to play.

It is important to understand that Swan was not guilty of taking a bribe or of match fixing but was charged with 'conspiracy to fraud a bookmaker', which he pleaded not guilty to, unlike Layne who pleaded guilty. The case was eventually brought before Nottingham Assizes in January 1965. Peter arrived for court with his solicitor Mr Arnold, who put the wind up him saying, 'Are you ready for prison?'

Peter Swan, along with Layne and Kay, was found guilty of fraud and all three were sentenced to four months in jail, initially in Lincoln. In sentencing, Judge Mr Justice Lawton, hearing the case, reflected the view of many involved in the game:

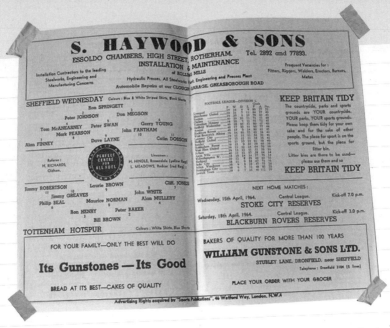

'I have to think of the tens of thousands of ordinary citizens who find relaxation in football and watching football. Over the years they paid their shillings to see a football match played as they thought by experts. For those shillings, they got not a match, but a dishonest charade. It is my duty to make it clear to other evil-minded persons in all kinds of sport that this is a serious crime. As internationals you should have been able to protect yourselves against any blandishments that might have been held out to you.'

And with that Swan was led to the cells – an international footballer with four young sons.

There was some support for Peter as there was a view that three punishments (fine, prison and a life ban) for one crime was unduly harsh and severe, and it was considered tragic that the draconian life ban was for a crime that earned him just over a month's wages, and it is also true the three high-profile stars were very peripheral in the complex betting syndicate, but the authorities wanted to deter others and in retrospect it is clear they were made examples of.

Further punishment was exacted as upon release they were all banned 'sine-die' from all football matters, including watching their local Sunday teams, and fined £100 – the amount of their winnings.

After leaving prison, Swan made a living working in a bakery, a car showroom and a hardware shop. Eventually his ban was lifted after eight long years in 1972 and he returned to Sheffield Wednesday where he played another 15 fixtures at the start of 1972/73, before losing his place and leaving for a season at Bury, for whom he scored after three minutes after never finding the net in 300 fixtures for the Owls. Bury got promoted that season from Division Four with Swan at the heart of the side, but he left after only being offered a monthly contract.

Above: The court papers against Peter Swan.
Below: Swan with his solicitor.

After that he became a non-league manager in the summer of 1974 and with some success, taking Matlock Town to Wembley in the 1975 FA Trophy Final, beating the much-fancied Scarborough 4-0.

Swan left at the end of his second season in the hope of managing a Football League club, but the call never came and he went back to non-league in due course and after retirement from the game worked in the licensed trade for many years before retiring and writing a book in 2006, which is essential reading – *Setting the Record Straight* published by Tempus Publishing.

F.A. CHALLENGE TROPHY COMPETITION

FINAL

MATLOCK TOWN

VERSUS

SCARBOROUGH

SATURDAY, 26th APRIL, 1975   Kick-off 3 p.m.

WEMBLEY
STADIUM

OFFICIAL PROGRAMME 10p

Swan lived for the rest of his life regretting his mistake but never lost his love of the sport at which he was so bountifully gifted. It must never be forgotten that he was such a talented footballer and that mistake cost him eight years of his career in his pomp. This author leaves it up to the reader as to how history will judge Peter Swan. Whilst agreeing with every word the judge said, it is hoped the reader's judgement will contain a small degree of empathy.

Peter Swan today.

Chapter 10

West Bromwich Albion v Tottenham Hotspur

4 - 4

Kick-off: 3pm   **Venue: The Hawthorns**   **Attendance: 34,500**

Porter	1	Brown
⚽ Howe	2	Baker
G. Williams	3	Hopkins
Frazer	4	Marchi
Jones	5	Norman
Simpson	6	J. Smith
Foggo	7	C. Jones ⚽
Fenton	8	White
⚽ Kaye	9	R. Smith ⚽
⚽ Fudge	10	Greaves ⚽⚽
⚽ Clark	11	Dyson

The Managers
Jimmy Hagan   Bill Nicholson

Match Report

After two matches involving the Sheffield clubs, we come to our final two fixtures involving clubs from the West Midlands, and this was yet another compelling game, with drama and controversy, only in this case the drama came on the field, with the controversy coming off it before the game took place.

The controversy surrounded the Albion players who had briefly gone on strike in the days leading up to the fixture, in protest against the manager's insistence that the players still train in shorts despite the Arctic temperatures. The manager was Jimmy Hagan and we shall have an in-depth look at his distinguished career later in the chapter.

In the Albion ranks was future Arsenal and England coach Don Howe, a serious thinker about the game when he was a player and, after his playing days were over, as a visionary coach. Howe represented the players in the dispute, but the players did not let this issue affect them as they showed a lot of fight to come back from two goals down three times in this fixture, including two late goals to rescue a point from high-flying Spurs who had been one of England's best teams over the previous three years and were in the middle of one of the club's most successful periods.

Spurs had started the season on fire offensively, scoring 23 goals in their first five home fixtures, including a memorable 4-4 draw with Arsenal in October 1963 under the lights at Highbury. They would score 97 that season but concede 81 – high octane entertainment indeed. Spurs had also won a European trophy (the European Cup Winners' Cup) only six months previously, thumping Atletico Madrid 5-1 in the final in Rotterdam.

Don Howe – right-back and captain of West Bromwich Albion FC.

Tottenham Hotspur – European Cup Winners' Cup champions in 1963.

This was a superb Spurs team going forward with a galaxy of attacking talent but with perhaps some defensive weaknesses, typified by losing 2-7 at Blackburn and shipping four at Old Trafford in the second leg of the early rounds of the 1963/64 European Cup Winners' Cup, for which they qualified as holders.

Spurs came into the Boxing Day fixture lying second (they finished in fourth position) with Blackburn above them on goal difference only. For this fixture, Spurs were without three defensive stalwarts – no Mackay, Henry or Blanchflower – which weakened them considerably.

Albion were a successful club in that era – reaching the FA Cup semi-final in 1957 and finishing in the top five in the First Division between 1957/58 and 1959/60 – but they were less successful in the early 1960s. They finished tenth, ninth and 14th leading up to 1963/64 and had lost Bobby Robson in late 1962 following a wage dispute with Albion chairman Jim Gaunt – and that is a theme we will come back to in this chapter. Manager Archie Macaulay left and was replaced by Jimmy Hagan in April 1963 after he had transformed the fortunes at Peterborough United, and this was his first crack at the First Division.

West Bromwich Albion in 1963/64

Albion came into the fixture in 11th position and would go on to finish tenth – they had won three and drawn one of their last four fixtures and had not long previously beaten Aston Villa 4-3 in a thriller at the Hawthorns. They were in good form despite the players' grumblings about the manager's regime. In fact, the Christmas fixtures came in the middle of a run of eight unbeaten – they were solid and could beat anybody on their day – and the highlight of the second half of the season was a 4-2 victory versus high-flying Everton.

In front of 34,500 – which was about double the Baggies' average – and on another difficult surface, which was very greasy and often threw up slithers of mud, the players gave us another great spectacle. It was difficult for the bigger players to turn, and famed football reporter David Miller, in his piece, suspected it may be a day for the smaller attacking players, and that was the way it turned out.

Tottenham Hotspur, in white with navy shorts and socks, started the brighter, and the goalscoring genius Jimmy Greaves volleyed Spurs ahead after four minutes from Dyson's centre. The Baggies, in traditional navy stripes, hung in there and were awarded a penalty on 15 minutes

John White – a wonderfully elegant and gifted footballer who so tragically died just seven months after this fixture at the age of 27 when he was hit by lightning whilst sheltering under a tree at Crews Hill Golf Course in Enfield in July 1964.

when Norman handled a free kick he conceded by fouling the elusive winger Clive Clark – however, Don Howe blazed over the bar to waste that opportunity, which became worse for West Bromwich when White put Greaves clear down the right, he beat the covering Jones with ease, cut in and presented Bobby Smith with an open goal to double Spurs' advantage – 0-2.

Kaye headed in from a free kick by Graham Williams to keep Albion in the fixture, but almost immediately Jones headed home a centre from Dyson to restore the two-goal advantage for Spurs, but – in a breathless spell just before the interval – Clive Clark hit a sharp half-volley, which beat Brown, and it was 2-3 at half-time and those lucky enough to attend this holiday fixture had been royally entertained.

Greaves scored three minutes after the interval – scoring from close range in the box as three defenders were about to close him down (finding space in a crowded box was his speciality) and that made it 4-2 and you suspected Spurs were home and hosed – not so.

On the hour, Clive Clark – small and quick, a firecracker of a footballer – saw off a challenge by John Smith and crossed for the splendidly named Micky Fudge to score his first league goal to make it 3-4 and the atmosphere changed completely – Jimmy Greaves would later comment on the 'rip-roaring atmosphere'.

Shortly afterwards, and with the Baggies now in the ascendancy, Norman mis-headed a clearance and left Clive Clark through on goal, but he pulled the ball wide of a gaping target with Spurs keeper Brown nowhere. Albion continued to press and finally got their reward nine minutes from time when Marchi conceded a corner, and when it came into the box Don Howe headed the ball towards goal. The defender Hopkins blocked

Micky Fudge – a Bristolian who played for West Bromwich Albion in the 1960s and who scored his first Baggies goal on Boxing Day 1963.

it but somehow Howe managed to stay on his feet and lashed the loose ball high into the Spurs goal – 4-4 and the Birmingham Road end was in raptures. Spurs hung on for the remaining nine minutes and it was reported in the press of the day that they looked 'nothing like Championship contenders'.

So 4-4 it finished and everybody went home happy with the entertainment on offer – West Bromwich went on to finish tenth and continued in mid-table, or just above, for the rest of the 1960s – winning the two-leg League Cup in 1966 (and runners-up in 1967 in the first Wembley League Cup final) and so memorably won the FA Cup with a Jeff Astle goal versus Everton at Wembley in 1968.

Albion boss Hagan could spot a player and the 1964 signing of Astle from Notts County – where he had been a consistent scorer – was arguably one of the best signings in West Bromwich Albion's history. He became a Baggies legend with 174 goals in 361 fixtures over a decade (ultimately being known as 'The King' by Albion followers and his passing in 2002 was mourned by thousands).

Spurs finished in fourth, making it a consistent run from 1959/60 – third, first, third, second, fourth, sixth, eighth and third – and experienced success in the FA Cup in 1961, 1962 and 1967 and the ECWC in 1962/63 – wonderful consistency from this group of players under a fine manager in Mr Bill Nicholson. This Spurs team was one of the finest in their history, but sadly for them – despite some cup trophies and a decent side in the early 70s winning three cups – they have not been able to win the top flight since. With the benefit of a wonderful new stadium, perhaps their time will come soon.

Jimmy Greaves –
without question a
goalscoring genius.

The Albion had an interesting period just after this Boxing Day fixture with the players still effectively on strike, although that withdrawal of labour did not extend to missing fixtures, which would have hit the club hard. There is an unwritten rule amongst players that even if you are in dispute with your club – either as an individual or as a group – that if selected to play you give your best if, for no other reason, than to re-assure future employers that you have the right attitude to play. The strike rumbled on into early 1964 and was only eventually settled when Albion chairman Jim Gaunt got the parties to agree a compromise – the players would wear shorts after the first 15 minutes of a session after they had warmed up! We will cover more elements of this dispute in a piece on Don Howe later.

Jimmy Greaves scored two goals on this Boxing Day – two of the 357 top-flight goals he scored in an amazing career – 366 if you include the nine he scored in the top flight in Milan. He was without doubt a goalscoring genius, and it is possible that his record of goals will never be beaten, although, as I write, Harry Kane may have an outside chance if he stays healthy and in the Premier League.

Return Match

 **Tottenham Hotspur
0-2
West Bromwich Albion**

Date: 28 December   **Venue:** White Hart Lane   **Att:** 47,863

Both teams travelled south to North London to have another go, and 47,863 were in attendance to box off the Christmas Holiday fixtures. Albion were unchanged whilst Spurs made just one – Eddie Clayton coming in for John White.

If Spurs not winning at the Hawthorns was a surprise – especially with them having a two-goal cushion on three occasions – then the Baggies winning 2-0 at White Hart Lane was a shock.

Throughout the first half, Albion had to do a lot of defending but they really dug in and looked dangerous on the break occasionally. The teams went in at half-time with the game goalless.

Albion attacking the Spurs goal at White Hart Lane.

Albion score on the break in London to take the points.

However, a couple of second-half goals from Ronnie Fenton and Ken Foggo enabled the Baggies to travel back to the West Midlands with two more points and a successful 48 hours against one of the best teams in the league.

It was one of only two occasions when Spurs failed to score at home that season – perhaps they had their eye on the high-profile FA Cup fixture they were to play the following week versus Chelsea (a match that ended 1-1 at the Lane, before Chelsea won 2-0 in the replay on 8 January 1964 in front of 70,000 at Stamford Bridge).

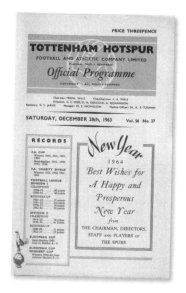

The manager for West Bromwich Albion for this period, and who made a contribution to the drama on Boxing Day – perhaps unwittingly and certainly unwillingly – was Jimmy Hagan, a very interesting character with a stellar career in both playing and coaching (see page 196).

PLAYER PROFILE
Donald Howe

Born on 12 October 1935 in Springfield, Wolverhampton, Howe was a high-quality defender, voted one of West Bromwich Albion's greatest-ever players and a visionary coach in his later career – arguably one of the best coaches we have ever had.

He attended St Peter's Collegiate School and showed promise as a footballer from an early age. He joined the ground staff at local club West Bromwich Albion in 1950, aged 15, and was invited to turn professional on his 17th birthday in 1952, but it would be another three years before he got on the pitch for the Baggies as a first-team player – he had to be patient. His debut was in the autumn of 1955 versus Everton, and he never looked back, giving almost a decade of service as one of the league's best right-backs – ultimately becoming captain – and he was a regular in the attractive Albion side that had three successive top-five finishes.

His style as a defender was not to dive in – he rarely completed a full tackle – preferring to use his football intelligence to intercept and jockey wingers into unfavourable positions to cross the ball.

Don Howe at West Brom.

With England captained by Billy Wright.

He was a thinking footballer and was soon to make his international debut in a 4-0 England win against Wales in Cardiff in October 1957, when he was just 22. He played in all four of England's fixtures in the 1958 World Cup in Sweden but sadly for him his last England appearance was in November 1959, aged just 24. In all, he played 23 times for England and was replaced at right-back by Jimmy Armfield, who ultimately competed with George Cohen for that slot in the run up to 1966.

After a decade of service featuring 340+ appearances, plus 23 international caps, Howe got a little unsettled in the summer of 1963, partly due to his salary of just £15 per week which was £5 less than the maximum wage that had been abolished two years earlier. At that time top footballers typically earned £35–£40 per week. There were six Albion players looking for a rise that summer, but Baggies chairman Gaunt was determined to hold out so Howe worked in the afternoons as a car salesman to boost his income.

West Bromwich Albion players walking out on strike on 20 December 1963.

Don had to sign a week-by-week contract in order for him to play in 1963/64, and he went into the season still an Albion player with a new manager to work with. New manager Hagan did not think his charges were fit enough and set about working them hard in the autumn of 1963, which Howe and his colleagues gradually resented – describing the Hagan regime as 'boring, authoritarian and tedious' – all resulting in them going on strike in December, when ten players asked for a transfer. Don Howe said, 'This is not a spontaneous reaction – it has been coming for a while – we want to be treated like adults.'

This era was breeding a slightly different footballer – free from the shackles of the maximum wage – and they felt more able to fight their corner. To be fair, much later, Howe did apologise to Jimmy Hagan saying he should have obeyed the manager's instructions.

It was almost time for Howe's career at The Hawthorns to close though, and he left in the summer of 1964 after 379 appearances and 19 goals from right-back – a really decent shift. He left for Arsenal for £42,000 and spent two years as a senior player and club captain – making 70 appearances before a broken leg versus Blackpool in 1966 effectively ended his playing career aged 31.

Don Howe, now in the colours of Arsenal, where he played for two seasons.

It was after his stellar playing career ended that Howe really rose to prominence as a high-class coach, but we should never forget how accomplished a player he was. He started his coaching career as reserve-team coach at Arsenal, working under Bertie Mee, and they were a perfect combination, with Howe being a track-suited, 'on-the-training-field coach' and Mee doing the rest. Shortly after, Howe stepped up to first-team coach when Dave Sexton left, and he – after some Wembley disappointments – was an integral part of the Arsenal set-up when they memorably beat Anderlecht under the lights at Highbury to win the 1970 Fairs Cup on a 4-3 aggregate, in a much-remembered fixture by Arsenal fans of a certain generation.

Howe then made a crucial contribution to Arsenal's double-winning team of 1970/71 – widely acknowledged to be the principal architect of that feat – and his stock was now high. He returned to The Hawthorns in 1971, but this time as the manager, as he had left on civil terms some seven years earlier.

HOWE QUITS ARSENAL

By HARRY MILLER

ALAN ASHMAN was sunning himself on a Greek island yesterday—with Arsenal coach Don Howe all set to replace him as manager of West Bromwich Albion.

He returns to Albion as the £9,000 chief

However, as often happens as coaching and management skills are quite different, his spell as a manager was not considered successful as the Baggies were relegated in his second season (1972/73), finishing bottom of the First Division with just nine wins, and he failed on two attempts to get them back – finishing eighth and sixth respectively – and he was sacked in 1975.

Howe had short spells with Leeds and Galatasaray before returning to Highbury in 1977 as head coach under former team-mate Terry Neill, and the Gunners made three cup finals and a European Cup Winners' Cup final, lost on penalties to Valencia. In 1981 Howe was also brought into the England set-up part-time by Ron Greenwood and retained by Bobby Robson.

After Neill was sacked in 1983, Howe got the manager's job after a caretaker period, but in his three-year spell at the helm Arsenal finished either sixth or seventh each season and he resigned at the end of the 1985/86 season – silverware was elusive for Arsenal in that period.

Howe with Bobby Robson.

Don Howe with
Terry Venables.

In 1987 he was requested by Bobby Gould to coach the 'Crazy Gang' at Wimbledon – a committed bunch of players – and he was the tactical brains behind them finishing seventh in the First Division and their unlikely FA Cup win in 1988, beating Liverpool at Wembley by using Dennis Wise to neutralise the effectiveness of John Barnes and designing the set piece that won the fixture for Wimbledon – a real career coaching highlight.

Don Howe became a 'coaching gun for hire' at this stage of his career – serving Bristol Rovers, QPR, Wimbledon again, Coventry and Chelsea in various capacities whilst working with England in the 1990 World Cup. He could not resist the offer from Terry Venables to work with England in 1995 as technical advisor, working with both the senior teams and the age groups, and he was a major contributor to that excellent England side that arguably should have won Euro 96 on home soil.

After that Don had his third stint with Arsenal as head of youth for six years – winning two FA Youth Cups before his semi-retirement in 2003, as he had some health issues. He continued to do some writing and media work until his passing in December 2015, aged 80. This author cannot improve on the words from Ivan Ponting in his obituary in *The Independent* –

'Don Howe gave his life to football, and few men have served the game with more keenness and care.'

PLAYER PROFILE
James Hagan

Born on 21 January 1918 in Washington, County Durham, Hagan was an outstanding footballer and a successful, if somewhat controversial, manager with an edge that was to cause as much conflict as it would bring successes in his life and career. As a player, he had magical ball skills and was both a provider and scorer of goals.

He was the son of Alfie Hagan, a professional footballer and coal miner with Newcastle United, Cardiff City and Tranmere Rovers. Initially, his wages were 10 shillings a week for working down the pit and £2 per week for playing for Newcastle United.

Young Jimmy had a tough upbringing in a mining community, with his father absent for long periods working the mines and furthering his football career. He often had to assume the 'man of the house' role and adopted a principled stance on many issues, including not going to a grammar school as they did not play football.

Alfie Hagan – miner and professional footballer from 1919–1927 – father of Jimmy Hagan.

Jimmy had a similar mentality to his father and they locked horns regularly, especially when over time it emerged that Jimmy – after trials for England Schools – was going to be the better footballer. Alfie struggled to deal with that and was continually abrasive and on occasion violent. On one occasion he punched the Catholic priest after a row, another time he killed Jimmy's favourite racing pigeon and he once destroyed all the images of Jimmy's fledging career – these experiences hardened young Jimmy to the outside world.

Jimmy left school at 14 and moved to Liverpool shortly after but came home after three months indicating he wanted to play football rather that work in a timber yard, as in those days apprentices worked in normal jobs in the afternoon, which young Jimmy was not a fan of.

He signed for Derby County as a 16-year-old and was playing in the first team by the age of 17, although he struggled a little to keep a regular slot as there were senior players blocking his way, but when he did play (seven goals in 30 appearances) he showed great promise and was spotted by Sheffield United manager Teddy Davidson.

After a disagreement with Derby boss George Dobey about his playing opportunities (the first of many conflicts in his

Jimmy Hagan.

career), Jimmy joined Sheffield United in 1938, aged just 20, for £2,500 and almost certainly he competes with Tony Currie as the best signing ever made by the Bramall Lane outfit.

Jimmy stayed with the Blades for 20 years and showed his incredible technique, goalscoring ability and levels of fitness, which stayed with him for the rest of his life.

After impressing the Blades faithful in his first few games and winning promotion at the end of his first season in 1938/39, his career was interrupted by the war, as were so many of that generation. However, he was selected for 16 wartime internationals (which were not decreed as full caps) and played alongside luminaries such as Matthews, Lawton and Carter.

Hagan meeting King George VI at Wembley in a wartime international versus Scotland in February 1944. Also in the picture are Stanley Matthews, Joe Mercer, Tommy Lawton and Cliff Britton. England won 6-2 with a memorable Hagan goal.

During the war, Jimmy was based in Aldershot, had risen to the rank of major in the army's Physical Training Corps – only being demobbed in 1946 – and he turned out for Aldershot in war fixtures with distinction and captained an Army XI in Germany in 1945. Even into his 50s Jimmy retained a high level of personal fitness and the disciplines learned in the army stayed with him for ever.

At the end of hostilities he resumed his club career and it is a real mystery how such a talented footballer who had performed with such distinction in war internationals only got one cap when they were deemed official – versus Denmark, away, on 26 September 1948 in a 0-0 draw.

There were a glut of gifted inside-forwards at the time – Carter, Mannion and Shackleton – but Hagan can still be considered unlucky, although the FA did present Hagan with an illuminated fames scroll covering his 14 war-time internationals.

The Blades finished sixth in the First Division in their first season back – 1946/47 – but finished bottom in 1948/49, despite Hagan's brilliance. However, he was able to help them back with promotion in 1952/53, finishing as Second Division champions, but his elegant brilliance could not prevent another relegation in 1955/56.

As his playing career began to develop its final phase, Jimmy finished playing in 1958 aged 40 – showing wonderful fitness and consistency – 361 fixtures and 117 goals in a 20-year spell for Sheffield United,

interrupted by six years of National Service. He is rightly regarded as a Blades Legend, although it is interesting to note the board did not recommend him for a management position at Bramall Lane.

Jimmy was given a testimonial in 1958 and this was a special evening. A good barometer of respect for a footballer is who comes back to play in a testimonial – especially in the pre-Premier League era.

SHEFFIELD XI	INTERNATIONAL XI
• Hodgkinson (Sheffield Utd)	• Harry Gregg (Man Utd & Ireland)
• Coldwell (Sheffield Utd)	• Jimmy Armfield (Blackpool & England)
• Makepeace (Doncaster Rovers)	• Alf McMichael (Newcastle & Ireland)
• Williams (Rotherham Utd)	• Danny Blanchflower (Spurs & Ireland)
• Shaw J. (Sheffield Utd)	• Billy Wright (Wolves & England)
• Keyworth (Rotherham Utd)	• Dave Bowen (Arsenal & Wales)
• Wilkinson (Sheffield Wed)	• Stanley Matthews (Blackpool & England)
• Quixall (Sheffield Wed)	• Jimmy Hagan (Sheffield Utd & England)
• Chappell (Barnsley)	• Brian Clough (Middlesbrough & England)
• Graham (Barnsley)	• Jimmy McIlroy (Burnley & Ireland)
• Hawksworth (Sheffield Utd)	• Tom Finney (Preston NE & England)

Just look at the International XI – a veritable who's who of superstar 1960s footballers. A sell-out 29,000 crowd watched the International XI win 4-3. It must have been a real treat on a bitterly cold night with snow on the pitch.

Peterborough United were a powerhouse in the Midland League in the late 1950s but had not played in the Football League up to that point. They appointed Hagan as manager in 1958 and he led the team to two more straight Midland League wins, and they were then elected into the Football League in 1960, replacing Gateshead, who suffered from poor attendances and were expensive to travel to.

The Posh (who attracted 10,000 even as a non-league club) then blitzed through Division Four breaking records with 134 goals in their first season, with Terry Bly scoring an incredible 52 alone – both records still standing today. They finished fifth in Division Three the next season with another 107 goals, but sadly Jimmy Hagan was sacked (after refusing to resign) in October 1962 after a bitter row with his new chairman and some of the players – seven of whom submitted transfer requests. It was a real shame after such a successful four years, which had not gone unnoticed amongst bigger clubs.

Jimmy Hagan joined First Division West Bromwich Albion in April 1963 and had a full pre-season to assess his squad, and he started to introduce some new training techniques – reducing the time from two hours to 90 minutes but making the training more physical with significantly more intensity.

Over the first half of the 1963/64 season, the players started to resent the 'inflexibility' of the training and, quote, 'the old-fashioned treatment of the players'. Their resentment boiled over when Hagan insisted on the players training in shorts during Arctic weather in December 1963. It also has to be said that Jimmy Hagan never – at any time in his coaching career – asked the players to do anything he could not do. The players refused to train and Jimmy Hagan trained initially on his own – in shorts – and then with the youth players. The dispute dragged on into 1964 but was ultimately settled with board intervention, and it must be emphasised that match performances and results did not suffer during this spell of player unrest.

Hagan also had a close shave during this time as, on Friday, 24 January 1964, just prior to facing Arsenal in an FA Cup fixture, his new car plunged 100 feet down a steep embankment, adjacent to the Baggies training ground in Spring Road, Smethwick.

It seems that Jimmy was getting used to his brand new Vauxhall Cresta's gearing when he left the car in reverse. When he started it the vehicle jumped back and he could not brake quickly enough and went down the bank. Hagan – just turned 46 – was able to crawl out of the smashed window as the car sank into the freezing cold waters of the Birmingham Canal but incurred cuts and bruises which necessitated a stay in hospital for two days and he missed the 3-3 draw against the Gunners.

Some of the Albion players leaving training at noon dashed over to help their manager – take a bow Simpson, Fenton, Williams and Jones – and after the club physio Dixon gave first aid, Hagan was stretchered up the bank, where he thanked his players at the top but noticed a couple were out of breath after running up the bank, so Jimmy suggested to them, without an ounce of humour, that they may wish to work on their fitness!

Hagan was taken to hospital but only after giving full instructions for the next day's fixture, including explanations to those that were to be left out, and, as an afterthought, to contact his wife. Thankfully Hagan made a full recovery.

Hagan, now with the goal threat of Jeff Astle, continued to build a decent side at West Bromwich despite these issues, and in 1965/66 they finished in the top six of the First Division and they won a trophy when they got all the way to the final of the League Cup after beating Peterborough in the semi-finals. This was the last season when the final was played over two legs and the Baggies beat West Ham 5-3 on aggregate after a memorable 4-1 second-leg win under the lights at The Hawthorns in March 1966.

However, despite that silverware, the following season – 1966/67 - was his final one as manager of West Bromwich Albion. The side once again reached the final of the League Cup – this time and forever now as a one-off Wembley showpiece final. They battered West Ham 6-2 in the semis over two legs, but despite leading Third Division Queens Park Rangers 2-0 in

Hagan (with tie) with West Bromwich Albion in 1965. By now, Don Howe had left for Arsenal but Jeff Astle had arrived – sat to Hagan's left – and was a superb signing.

the final, the Rodney Marsh-inspired Londoners came back to win 3-2. This was a serious disappointment to all concerned at West Bromwich and Jimmy Hagan's Albion career never really recovered.

Despite winning eight of the last 12 fixtures and finishing mid-table, Jimmy Hagan was sacked by West Bromwich Albion in summer 1967 and he would never again manage in the country of his birth. In a more recent Q&A Graham Williams indicated that Hagan was a magician with a football and often wanted to take part in training, and he was ferocious in the dressing room if players did not do as he asked whilst being good company out of work – although Hagan was teetotal.

His severance package was sufficiently generous for him to invest in a driving school and he kept in touch with football by working for the Pools Panel, doing some coaching at clinics in Lilleshall and some scouting for Manchester City, but he was out of front-line management for three years when he got the call that changed his life. SL Benfica from Lisbon

– one of Europe's finest clubs at that point – were perceived to be in a bit of a slump with some complacency (not going on to win the league in 1969/70) and they felt they needed an English-style disciplinarian manager to give them fresh focus and structure.

They tried for Alf Ramsey but were rebuffed as Alf was busy preparing to take England to Mexico and a third party, Charlie Mitten, suggested Jimmy Hagan – and he went to Lisbon to join Benfica in February 1970 with an unusual contract. Hagan was to be paid just a salary and had to sort out his own house and car but was to have complete control on training, recruitment and selection. It must also be remembered that coaches in Portugal tended to last one year – all four before Jimmy did and the three after him and just did the coaching.

Hagan – as ever – decided the players were nowhere near fit enough and set about shaping his team and it will not be a surprise to the readers when he soon had the players running up and down the steps at the Estadio da Luz to develop some basic fitness and Hagan at 50+ led the sessions. It was reported that many players were physically sick after some of the early sessions but they soon realised that results improved as they were fitter and stronger and three years of wonderful success followed.

Benfica won the league in each of Hagan's three full seasons – in 1971/72 they lost just once and in 1972/73 they went one better and progressed through the whole season unbeaten – winning 28 of the 30 fixtures and scoring 101 goals in the process, including 43 by the revitalised and fitter Eusebio (at that point 31 years old). Even allowing for the variable quality of some of the opposition, this was a remarkable achievement by Hagan and this group of players.

There were some disappointments in Europe, including losing over two legs to Derby County in the European Cup, but the Hagan era in Lisbon made him an unlikely hero and he was regularly mobbed in the streets of the Portuguese capital. When the end came for Hagan in Lisbon it was not a football decision.

In September 1973 at Eusebio's testimonial Jimmy insisted on the players doing normal league match preparation, otherwise they would not be picked – some did but three did not and Hagan de-selected them. The chairman overruled Jimmy and when he saw them warming up Hagan felt his authority and control had been compromised – in breach of his contract – and he walked out of the stadium, never to return.

A tearful Eusebio went to Jimmy's home to persuade him to attend the after-match dinner – which he did out of respect for a player he admired – but that was it for Hagan at Benfica. As ever Jimmy showed his principles.

Hagan worked thereafter in Estoril, winning the Third Division, at Al-Arabi in Kuwait, Sporting Lisbon, finishing second behind Benfica, and enjoyed short spells with smaller Portuguese clubs, one of which was Boavista in Porto, with whom he won the Portuguese Cup – a big shock.

Jimmy Hagan – dark suit – with the Benfica team.

Jimmy came back to England eventually and passed away in 1998 aged 80 after spending his last two years in a nursing home just a couple of miles away from Bramall Lane – the ground where his star shone so brightly.

You need to be a special footballer to have a statue at the ground you graced for 20 years – this statue of Jimmy Hagan is in the ticket office at Bramall Lane and it is an indication of the affection that Eusebio had for him that he travelled from Lisbon to unveil it in 2001 – Jimmy Hagan had revitalised Eusebio's career in the early 1970s.

Jimmy Hagan – gifted footballer, effective coach and highly principled man – revered in Sheffield, West Bromwich and Lisbon.

Rest In Peace, Sir.

Chapter 11

Wolverhampton Wanderers v Aston Villa

3 - 3

Kick-off: 3pm   **Venue: Molineux**   **Attendance: 27,569**

Barron	1	Sims
Showell	2	Wright
Thompson	3	Aitken
Goodwin	4	V. Crowe ⚽
Flowers	5	Sleeuwenhoek
Kirkham	6	Deakin
⚽ Wharton	7	MacEwan
C. Crowe	8	Ewing
⚽⚽ Crawford	9	Hateley ⚽
Broadbent	10	Pountney ⚽
Hinton	11	Burrows

The Managers

Stan Collis   Joe Mercer

Match Report

Throughout the 1950s Wolverhampton Wanderers had been an outstanding side with one of the best teams in the history of English club football. Under Stan Cullis, who had been appointed in 1948 aged just 31, having played for the club either side of World War Two, they dominated the 1950s and enjoyed some memorable evenings under the Molineux floodlights against top-quality continental opposition.

Cullis was to become the most successful manager in Wolves' history with some visionary methods – placing huge emphasis on fitness and power – playing long balls into space to allow strong runners to attack. Cullis built the team that won its first title in 1953/54, with players such as Wright, Slater, Hancocks and goalkeeper Williams.

They followed this by coming second, third and sixth before winning the title again in 1957/58. There is no doubt they were the best side from 1957 to 1960, retaining their title in 1958/59 and coming second to surprise winners Burnley in 1959/60, depriving Cullis of the double by one point as Wolves won the FA Cup that season.

Right:
Wolves v Spartak Moscow,
16 November 1954.

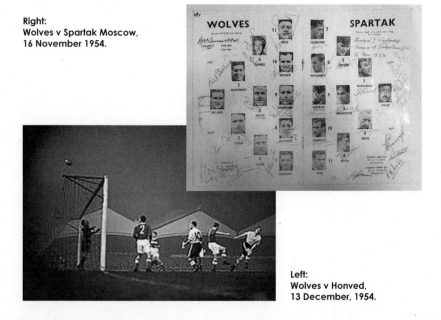

Left:
Wolves v Honved,
13 December, 1954.

Wolverhampton Wanderers in 1963/64.

This was a free-scoring outfit too – scoring 103 in 42 fixtures in 1957/58 as new players came in – Flowers, Deeley and Broadbent. They scored another 100 in 1958/59 and 106 in 1959/60.

Wolves finished third in 1960/61 but that was as good as it got for them in that era, and they finished 18th in 1961/62 before mounting a modest revival to get back in the top five in 1962/63, but the group was aging and needed some refreshing.

Wolves approached the 1963/64 season with some optimism, still under Stan Cullis with some new players, and once again there was plenty of action with 46 goals in their first ten fixtures – losing 4-3 at Spurs, 6-0 at Liverpool, and suffering home defeats to Blackburn (5-1) and Spurs (4-1), but they did secure a morale-boosting 4-1 home win against Chelsea.

Wolves picked up a bit as Christmas approached – winning at Leicester and beating Manchester United at Molineux – coming into the Boxing Day fixture in 14th position.

Aston Villa were omnipresent in the First Division throughout the 1950s, flirting with the top four a couple of times and with relegation too. They also managed to win the FA Cup in 1957, beating the pre-Munich Manchester United – their first trophy for 37 years.

However, Villa were relegated in 1958/59 as the decade came to an end – manager Eric Houghton was sacked and his replacement Joe Mercer was unable to keep them up – being relegated with Portsmouth. Villa historians regard this season as one of complacency as the talent was there – getting to the semi-finals of the FA Cup was indicative of that talent – losing to Forest by the only goal in the semi-final – and this was only the second relegation in Villa's long and rich history.

However, Villa returned straight away, winning the Second Division in 1959/60 – with 25 wins – and coming up with Cardiff City and again reaching the semi-finals in the FA Cup. Again, they lost 1-0, this time to Wolves. Villa settled back in to the top flight quickly in 1960/61 and finished ninth and won the inaugural League Cup – beating Rotherham 3-2 after extra time over two legs. Villa then had finishes of seventh and 15th and came into 1963/64 optimistic that they could push on and arrest the decline, but they were to finish in the bottom four, which cost manager Mercer his job.

The season started with a win on Trentside versus Forest, but two successive home defeats to Stoke and Blackburn gave a clue that perhaps it might be a struggle. As was often the case this season with all clubs, there were plenty of goals about – Villa won 4-0 at Blackpool but lost 4-2 at home to Spurs, 5-2 at Anfield versus Liverpool and 4-3 at West Bromwich Albion. A run of four straight losses in late September and October sent Villa down the table and they came into Boxing Day on a run of only four wins in 14 fixtures and sat in 17th place at the start of play that afternoon.

The conditions underfoot were officially described as heavy, and moving the ball quickly was a problem for the players. Villa started the brighter and tested the Wolves keeper Jim Barron regularly in the first 20 minutes. He saved a 20-yarder from Tony Hateley and then almost conceded an own goal. On 22 minutes the Villa attacker Pountney seemed to have opened the scoring but the goal was disallowed for offside by referee Mr Crawford, which left all 22 players perplexed. Still it was all Villa at this stage and on the half hour Ewing hit the underside of the bar, but it stayed out and Barron then somehow saved a shot from Burrows without knowing too much about it.

So, no goals at half-time, and as the players trooped down the tunnel the *Express and Star* reported that, 'Villa must have felt that Santa Claus must have crossed them off his list.'

Wolves were still 'ragged' according to local reports in the early stages of the second half, and everybody was waiting for the inevitable Villa goal – and that sense of injustice worsened when on 55 minutes Wolves took the lead. Wolves right-winger Terry Wharton evaded Aitken for probably the first time in the fixture, got clear and shot low and hard under the diving Sims – 1-0 to the Wanderers and the North Bank celebrated. It was to be only six minutes later when they could celebrate again as Ray Crawford scored with his knee from a Wharton cross from the right and – would you believe it – 60 seconds later the enigmatic Crawford scored again, but this time from an Alan Hinton cross from the left.

Just over an hour played and Villa were having the better of the play – yet they found themselves 3-0 down with less than 30 minutes to go. They recovered their composure and began to get a grip on the fixture and threatened the Wolves goal when Showell cleared off the Wolves goal line.

Aston Villa in 1963/64.

An Aston Villa goal was looking inevitable and it arrived on 71 minutes when Dave Pountney forced the ball home from close range after a scramble in the goal when a ball rebounded from Aitken. Five minutes later, a corner from the left by Burrows was headed on by Deakin to the feet of Vic Crowe and the Villa skipper made no mistake again from close range – 3-2 with 14 minutes left and Aston Villa were most certainly in the ascendancy now.

Villa pounded the Wolves goal. Hateley should have scored with a header and then shot directly at Barron when it looked easier to score and then Barron made an agile save from a shot by Burrows – breathless stuff and the elusive equaliser just would not come … until in the final minute another corner from Burrows was headed home by the tall Hateley to give Aston Villa a point, which was the minimum they deserved on this particular afternoon.

The 27,000 in attendance that muddy afternoon in Wolverhampton applauded both teams off the pitch. Glorious entertainment in the second half with six goals and a host of near misses – 'well done to both teams' was the sentiment from the local press representing both sides. Could the same group of players entertain so royally 48 hours later, just a short journey away in Aston?

Return Match

Aston Villa
2-2
Wolverhampton Wanderers

Date: 28 December **Venue:** Villa Park **Att:** 34,029

The Boxing Day fixture at Molineux was the second instance in this block of fixtures that an away team had come back from being 3-0 down and had drawn level in the last minute – that normally happens a couple of times per season – but on this Boxing Day it happened twice. What would the return fixture have in store?

There were 34,029 at Villa Park that afternoon – no doubt hoping to be as royally entertained as those present at Molineux. The famous old ground in Birmingham was very muddy but saw both sides battle out another thrilling draw, with Villa once again coming from behind twice to gather a share of the spoils.

The fixture was evenly matched and on 21 minutes Ray Crawford opened the scoring with a crisp half-volley past the diving Sims in the Villa goal at the Holte End.

The lively Villa winger Burrows equalised on 32 minutes when he latched on to a centre from Ewing to score and the teams were once again level at half-time.

Crowe restored Wolves' advantage just after the break with a goal on the counter attack, but three minutes later Burrows scored a wonderful goal in front of the cavernous Holte End terrace, volleying home a corner from MacEwan from the right which screamed in the top corner and finished the scoring for the afternoon – although Pountney spoiled a hard-working performance for Villa by spurning a couple of chances to win the fixture late on. Two exciting fixtures for the Midlands football fans to enjoy – ten goals, two comebacks and honours shared.

It was not to be a vintage season though for either of these two clubs – Aston Villa finished 19th and in the bottom four whilst Wolves ended just three places higher in 16th.

Villa went on to struggle for the next two seasons in the bottom half and were in fact relegated to the Second Division in 1966/67 – going down with Blackpool – and their decline was such that they had two mediocre seasons in that division before being relegated again to the Third Division in season 1969/70, along with Preston.

The 1960s and early 1970s was a turbulent time for Villa with many changes of playing and managerial personnel along with significant activity in the boardroom.

They took two seasons to get out of the Third Division, but it was a very enjoyable season with record crowds for that level – one game versus Bournemouth attracted a fantastic attendance of 49,000.

Aston Villa then began the long climb back, which culminated so memorably with the First Division championship in 1980/81 followed by the European Cup 12 months later – a talented team indeed, including Mortimer, Withe, Shaw, Evans and Morley.

Wolverhampton Wanderers also fell a bit in the mid-60s, actually being relegated the following season with Birmingham City – a season when they bizarrely sold their top scorer Ray Crawford to their local rivals. Wolves did manage to get back after two seasons, being promoted with Coventry City in 1966/67 – the end-of-season fixture between the two to determine the title (won by the Sky Blues) attracted 51,000 to Highfield Road.

Wolves were comfortable in mid-table but were building a side that finished fourth in 1971, with Dougan and Richards up front, but they never threatened after that and went down again in 1976, came back, were relegated in 1982, came back, were relegated in 1984 and then sadly fell away with two more successive relegations to leave them in the Fourth Division with some serious financial issues caused, in part, by the construction of a superb stand. Once again turbulent times in the West Midlands.

However, Wolves then signed a young striker from West Bromwich Albion called Steve Bull in 1986 and he inspired them to climb back to the second tier with 306 goals in 13 seasons, and as I write they are back in the top flight performing well in the famous Old Gold kit.

PLAYER PROFILE
Raymond Crawford

Born on 13 July 1936 in Portsmouth, Ray Crawford was a top player with over 300 career club goals in under 500 fixtures.

He was one of four children born in a small flat in Fratton Road, Portsmouth, just over a long free-kick away from Fratton Park. He started his football career as a trainee at his home-town club. Ray's father was a professional boxer and he inherited his father's build and athleticism, although Ray did suffer from asthma a bit as a youth.

He was playing for a local side, Sultan Boys, in 1952 as a 16-year-old when selected to play for the Portsmouth youth-team at Fratton and caught the eye of some of the first-team players. Ray was put on a retainer of £1 per week at Portsmouth as he began his National Service in 1954, after starting work making concrete and breeze blocks for Portsmouth Trading Company.

After his service, and many football fixtures, in Egypt and Malaya, amongst others – earning them the nickname 'Jungle Boy' – Ray returned to the UK and resumed his career at Portsmouth. He eventually made his debut on 24 August 1957 versus Burnley, which finished goalless – Ray had just turned 22. His Portsmouth career really ignited the next fixture against the mighty Spurs who would finish third that year. Ray scored twice in two minutes as Pompey won 5-1 in one of the most memorable evenings of his career.

Portsmouth lost the next fixture 4-0 at Preston and finished third from bottom in 1957/58, sacking manager Eddie Lever as a result. But the young Crawford scored nine times in 17 fixtures and appeared to have a positive future ahead of him at Fratton Park. He was fond of the outgoing manager, who informed his replacement Freddie Cox to 'keep Crawford as he will play for England' – a prediction that came true.

However, just three fixtures into the 1958/59 season, Crawford was inexplicably sold to Ipswich Town – a league below Pompey at the time – one of the most controversial transfers in the history of Portsmouth FC. In searching for some retrospective rationale, it seems the new manager Cox and chairman Sparshatt did not rate Crawford and there may have been some financial pressures.

Crawford left for Ipswich with massive reluctance – Portsmouth was his home-town club, he was newly married, just moved home and expecting his first child. It is important to note that, two seasons later, Portsmouth were in Division Three as the replacements for Ray and others were not of the quality required to keep Pompey in the top flight … or the Second Division.

Retrospectively, it was a good time to join Ipswich, who were about to embark on a sporting romantic journey of promotion to the First Division in 1960/61 and the title the following season under Alf Ramsey – the first club to achieve that.

Crawford in action for Ipswich Town.

Ipswich Town – First Division title winners 1961/62.

Crawford was an integral part of that amazing journey never to be forgotten in Suffolk. He scored 26 goals in 33 appearances in his first season and then 18 in 37 in his second and 40 in 44 in his third, as Ipswich swept through the Second Division with 100 goals scored.

The magical season to follow has gone down in football folklore. Ipswich won the First Division title as a newly promoted club – scoring 93 goals – winning 24 of their 42 fixtures, with Crawford scoring 37 goals in 50 appearances in all competitions.

The critics had Ipswich down as relegation certainties, but it was a magical season and Ipswich just kept picking up points. After only getting one draw from their first three fixtures, they beat Burnley 6-2 in the fourth game and never looked back.

Crawford developed a successful partnership with Ted Phillips at Portman Road and finished that season with 33 league goals – joint top scorer that season with Derek Kevan of West Bromwich Albion.

Ray Crawford playing for England in 1962

Despite being a major part of the title-winning side, and a consistent goal scorer, Crawford was only picked for England twice. Firstly versus Northern Ireland in 1961 and the next fixture against Austria in 1962 when he opened the scoring in a 3-1 win. He did not travel to Chile for the World Cup and never played again for his country, even though his Ipswich Town manager Alf Ramsey took the reins in 1963.

Crawford played for Ipswich for two more seasons (with more goals) but it was never the same after Ramsey left for the England job in 1963, and he left for Wolves in September that same year – just as Ipswich were sliding towards relegation and just before their record defeat at Fulham.

He stayed at Wolves for 18 months – with more goals – before a brief spell at West Bromwich. He then returned to Ipswich in 1966 for another three seasons, ending up with 227 goals in 353 fixtures – amazing consistency.

The second spell included another promotion back to the top flight in 1967/68, which rightly instilled Ray Crawford as an East Anglian legend. He then had a spell with Charlton and some time with

Kettering Town before an enjoyable 'Indian summer' season with Colchester United (1970/71 and another 31 goals). He was once again in the national spotlight when the Essex club drew mighty Leeds United in the FA Cup at their modest Layer Road ground, beating them 3-2 with the irrepressible Crawford scoring twice.

Manager Dick Graham had spotted that Gary Sprake was sometimes unsure whether to come for crosses, and from a set piece a ball was placed between the goal line and the six-yard box and Ray scored with a powerful header. His second goal was bizarre – he was on the ground and managed to hook a loose ball towards the goal. It bobbled against the post and went in.

After a season in South Africa, Ray retired from playing, moving into coaching and management roles with Brighton (leaving when Brian Clough arrived), Portsmouth and in non-league with Fareham and Winchester.

He worked as a merchandising representative and more recently in local radio in Portsmouth and Suffolk, which he excels at with his ebullient personality.

Ray with a framed picture of the first of those famous goals against Leeds United.

He published his memoirs in 2007 – an excellent read about a decent career which included two promotions, winning the First Division, playing for and scoring for England, and scoring 300 goals in 500 fixtures.

As I write, Ray Crawford is 83, living in his beloved Portsmouth and still active, doing radio and supporting charities.

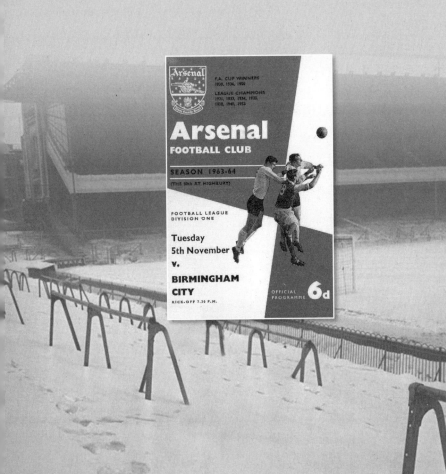

Chapter 12

Arsenal v Birmingham City

4 - 1

Kick-off: 3pm   **Venue: Highbury**   **Attendance: 23,499**

Wilson	1	Withers
Neill	2	Lynn
Clarke	3	Green
Magill	4	Hennessey
Brown	5	Smith
Anderson	6	Hellawell
Barnwell	7	Auld
MacLeod	8	Bloomfield ⚽
⚽⚽⚽ Baker	9	Beard
Eastham	10	Harley
⚽ Strong	11	Bullock

The Managers

Billy Wright   Gill Merrick

Match Report

20 of the 22 First Division clubs played on Boxing Day as the weather was just about OK for games to take place, but the conditions, at best, were heavy, or, at worst, treacherous, as we have seen up and down the country. The two teams that didn't play were Arsenal and Birmingham City as their scheduled Boxing Day fixture had been brought forward to 5 November to allow Arsenal flexibility regarding their Inter Cities Fairs Cup fixtures due in December, thus preventing a fixture pile-up. They played against Liege in Belgium on 18 December and had a First Division fixture on 21 December. The original return fixture was played as scheduled on 28 December, so to be fair to the two clubs we'll cover their matches too.

Arsenal went into the game in great form. At Highbury, in their previous three home fixtures, they had put six past Ipswich and four past both Spurs (in a 4-4 draw, in front of 67,000) and Nottingham Forest.

Birmingham had won the League Cup the previous season, memorably beating rivals Aston Villa 3-1 over a two-leg final, to win their first-ever trophy. However, they finished in the bottom three in the league that season and they struggled once again coming in to 1963/64, seemingly not able to generate any consistency with endless team changes in a vain attempt to capture some rhythm. In all, 25 players were used, with

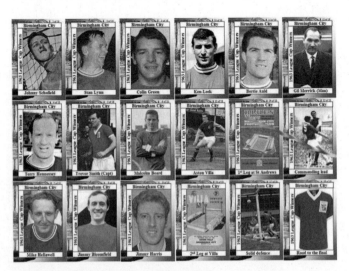

Birmingham City, 1962/63 League Cup winners.

Arsenal in 1963/64

15 different goalscorers, which gives you an idea of their fragmented selection. Typical of the Blues' season was an FA Cup defeat at home to Third Division Port Vale and a League Cup defeat to Norwich City from Division Two. Despite beating Bolton in their opening fixture, they lost nine of their next 12, including shipping six at Spurs, but strangely had won 3-2 at Chelsea on the Saturday before this re-arranged fixture.

Arsenal won this game with comfort against a below-par Birmingham City after being 2-1 up at half-time, temporarily going top of the table with 32 points from 17 fixtures, although the chasing pack all had games in hand. Joe Baker scored a hat-trick and Geoff Strong also claimed, with Jimmy Bloomfield (a former Arsenal player) getting a consolation for Birmingham. This win kept up their impressive scoring streak at home. Later that same week they drew 3-3 with West Ham at Highbury in front of 52,000 and two weeks later beat Blackpool 5-3 – great entertainment in North London.

Arsenal, under Billy Wright, went on to finish eighth, fading a bit from what was a promising position. However, they were wonderful going forward, scoring 90 goals – only champions Liverpool (92) and fellow North Londoners Spurs (97) scored more. Conversely, only two of the bottom three had a worse defensive record. They had a disappointment in the Inter Cities Fairs Cup – going out to Liege of Belgium 4-2 over two legs.

Birmingham were poor that evening and not much better at any other time during that season, finishing one spot above the relegation places.

Return Match

Birmingham City
1-4
Arsenal

Date: 28 December   **Venue:** St Andrew's   **Att:** 23,337

With the fixture being seven weeks after their first meeting, there were a number of changes. The Blues brought in Bobby Thomson and Ken Leek, whilst the Gunners had Jim Furnell in goal, with Ian Ure and John Snedden defensively, and George Armstrong on the flank.

Arsenal prevailed once again by the same scoreline after being 2-1 ahead at the interval. Goals from George Armstrong, Joe Baker and two from Johnny MacLeod did for the Blues, who responded with a consolation from Scot Alex Harley in front of a crowd of 23,337.

The defeat left Birmingham in 19th place and they were to finish in 20th, with manager Gil Merrick leaving at the end of the season. Bertie Auld (later a Celtic legend), with just ten goals, was the top scorer and only Bolton scored fewer goals that season in the First Division.

They had a bad run from 1 February, losing eight out of nine games, including shipping five at Wolves.

Bertie Auld – Birmingham City and Scotland.

They survived relegation by winning their final two fixtures, both at St Andrew's, firstly against champions elect Liverpool 3-1 and finally 3-0 against Sheffield United in front of 26,000, which kept them up for another season.

Sadly, however, they finished bottom the following season with only eight wins despite the change of manager and it was to be another seven years before they returned to the top flight.

Arsenal were in the middle of legendary player Billy Wright's stewardship, which has not been considered a success by Arsenal historians. After finishing eighth in 1963/63 with an entertaining team but one which conceded goals alarmingly, the following two seasons saw them finish 13th and 14th, with Wright leaving the club in the summer of 1966.

Chapter 13

The Boys of '66
– Where Were They in '63?

In December 1963 we were just two-and-a-half years from the greatest day in English football history when England won the World Cup on 30 July 1966. It is therefore timely to review where they were on their journey to immortality and whether they made a contribution to this special Boxing Day?

Football fate is fickle. In December 1963 it would have been impossible to select the England team that would contest the World Cup. Perhaps we would have chosen a core consisting of Bobby Moore, Bobby Charlton, Ray Wilson, Gordon Banks and almost certainly Jimmy Greaves. After that you would not have picked, with any degree of certainty, any of the others who did eventually play.

It is interesting to note that two defensive mainstays of the side were not playing in the top flight in December 1963 and, with 30 months to go, six players had not even made their debuts for England. Firstly, let us document the 11 players who were on the pitch that memorable afternoon in 1966, along with their manager. Players are listed in squad number order.

1. Gordon Banks

He played for Leicester v Everton and had been England's regular keeper since making his debut earlier that year. He made 73 appearances for England between 1963 and 1972. He continued to play for Leicester until 1967 when the prodigious emerging talent of Peter Shilton persuaded the Leicester City board to sell Banks to Stoke City, which hurt him hugely at the time. His career was finished in England as a result of  an eye injury in a car crash in October 1972. Gordon Banks passed away in February 2019 aged 81.

2. George Reginald Cohen

Cohen played for Fulham that afternoon as right-back in the 10-1 win v Ipswich. Back in 1963 he had yet to play for England, not making his international debut until 1964 aged 25. He played until 1967, making 37 appearances. Cohen was a one-club man with 459 league appearances for Fulham over 13 years (1956–69). He was a Fulham player for eight years and first played for England at the age of 25.

3. Ramon Wilson

Wilson was not playing in the First Division in 1963/64 – he was in his 12th and final season for Huddersfield in the Second Division, although he had made his England debut in 1960 and remains Huddersfield's most capped international footballer. He joined Everton in the summer of 1964 but missed most of his first season with a torn thigh muscle. He had five seasons with the Toffees. Wilson played 63 times for his country  over eight years and was the regular left-back for much of that time. He was the oldest player in the 1966 team at 31 but regarded by many as England's best-ever defensive left-back. Perhaps the lowest profile member of the 1966 team, and Wilson would have wanted it that way. Wilson passed away in May 2018, aged 83.

4. Norbert Peter Stiles

Stiles was with Manchester United that afternoon but didn't play due to injury. He made 395 appearances in all competitions for United over 11 years. However, in 1963 he had yet to make his England debut, which came in 1965. Alf Ramsey explained that Stiles was picked as a 'spoiler', allowing Bobby Charlton the space to play – a role that Stiles performed to perfection as he was a fine combative midfielder. He won 28 England caps over five years (the least capped of the '66 team) and wasn't selected after 1967. Now aged 77, he lives in Manchester but is suffering from dementia.

5. John Charlton

Known as 'Jack', Charlton was getting promoted to Division One that season with Leeds United under Don Revie. Another one-club man, Jack played centre-half for Leeds for 21 seasons until aged 37, making 762 appearances, scoring 95 goals. He was almost 30 when he made his England debut v Scotland in 1965 and was picked alongside Bobby Moore to provide cover, as Moore often came forward with the ball. Jack played his 35th and final game for England in 1970 v Czechoslovakia in the World Cup. After a distinguished career as a manager with several clubs and the Republic of Ireland, Jack retired in 1996 and lives in Northumberland, now aged 84.

6. Robert Frederick Chelsea Moore

Moore played for West Ham in their Boxing Day fixture v Blackburn Rovers – one of 647 fixtures for the Hammers in all competitions. A Rolls-Royce of a footballer, he played a total of 795 club fixtures and 108 times for his country over 11 years, captaining the national team from 1963 aged just 22. He was Alf Ramsey's much-respected leader on the pitch and one of England's greatest-ever footballers. Tragically, he was the first of the 1966 team to pass away, in February 1993, aged just 51 – a loss felt by millions, particularly in the East End of London where he remains an icon.

7. Alan James Ball

Ball played for Blackpool in 1963 but was injured for their Boxing Day game. Aged just 18 at the time, he played in 31 of Blackpool's games that season as inside-right, top scoring with 13 goals, often 'carrying' the team. He was still with Blackpool in the summer of 1966 after an impressive season (16 goals in 41 games). He joined Everton for the 1966/67 season. In total he scored 211 goals in 951 club appearances and had a decent 20-year managerial career over 650 games. The youngest of the 1966 team, he won 72 England caps over ten years. Alan Ball also passed away very young in 2007, aged 61.

9. Sir Robert Charlton

Charlton played for Manchester United that afternoon in their defeat at Burnley. Considered a legend of the game, Ramsey admitted that he built his World Cup team around him from an attacking perspective and around Bobby Moore from a defensive angle. Charlton played over 800 club games, the vast majority for United, scoring 260 goals. He won 106 caps over 12 years, scoring 49 goals. Sir Bobby lives in Manchester, aged 81, and is still heavily involved with his beloved Manchester United.

10. Sir Geoffrey Charles Hurst

Geoff played for West Ham that Boxing Day and, by all accounts, did not have his best day, missing a number of chances. Thankfully for Hurst, there were more good days than bad ones in a fantastic career, highlighted by that hat-trick at Wembley. A veteran of 674 club fixtures largely for West Ham and Stoke, Hurst scored 299 club goals and 24 international goals (from 49 caps) in a seven-year England career, although his first cap did not come until April 1966 at Hampden Park. The quarter-final v Argentina, when he scored the decisive goal, was in fact only his second cap - a late developer indeed for the World Cup XI. Hurst is now retired, aged 77, and living in Cheltenham.

16. Martin Stanford Peters

Peters played for West Ham United in their heavy defeat at home to Blackburn Rovers on Boxing Day 1963 and was dropped for the return fixture at Ewood Park, in favour of the more combative Eddie Bovington. An elegant footballer with precise passing skills and great movement, making him difficult to mark, Peters had a stellar playing career with West Ham, Tottenham Hotspur, Norwich City and, briefly, Sheffield United, amassing over 800 appearances and 67  England caps (over eight years). He was the scorer of 'the other goal' in the final. Sadly, Peters passed away in December 2019, aged 76.

21. Roger Hunt

Hunt played for Liverpool that day, scoring four times in a 6-1 win v Stoke City. Hunt was a much under-rated footballer, who was a late developer in the professional game. He was a wonderful servant to the sport and his career is covered in much more detail in the narrative (see page 141). Roger is now 81 years old and living in retirement in Warrington.

Manager – Sir Alfred Ernest Ramsey

He had a successful career as a player and took Ipswich to an unlikely First Division championship in 1961/62 as a manager and was appointed England manager in October 1962. He didn't actually didn't take charge until May 1963, so by December 1963 he would have been starting to plan his World Cup campaign. He memorably predicted an England win in 1966 when pressed by a journalist. Sir Alf passed away in 1999, aged 79.

The Squad Players

8. James Peter Greaves

Greaves scored two for Tottenham at West Bromwich Albion on Boxing Day 1963 in a 4-4 draw.

He was without doubt the most high-profile absentee from the England starting XI that July afternoon. He was the outstanding goalscorer of his generation – in fact, of any generation – with 366 top-flight goals in two European countries. However, some football historians believe that, even with an outstanding scoring record for club and country, Sir Alf Ramsey was never 100 per cent committed to his style of play, as he was a 4-1-3-2 man with limited width, whilst Greaves was a bit maverick, often dropping into space outside of the team shape. As a result, Greaves had been dropped a couple of times before the finals.

Greaves had missed some of season 1965/66 with hepatitis but scored four against Norway in a warm-up fixture and played in England's three group fixtures, but he was not particularly effective and picked up an injury (a cut shin requiring stitches). These two factors combined to keep him out for the rest of the tournament – opening the door for Geoff Hurst.

Greaves was fit for the final and his exclusion from the biggest fixture in his life was a massive blow to him and one which – according to his book – along with the sad passing of his infant son, contributed to the depression and alcoholism problems he had when he stopped playing – not helped by the fact that only those who played got medals, although this was corrected many years later.

His England career fizzled out after 1966 with only three more appearances, and he was never quite the same player again. He finished with 44 goals in 57 appearances.

He continued to score First Division goals for six more seasons, but his form gradually fell away in the late 60s before a move to West Ham, which he regretted.

11. John Michael Connelly

Connelly played for Burnley against Manchester United, winning 6-1, and won 20 caps for England as a winger.

12. Ronald Deryk George Springett

Springett was a goalkeeper who played for Sheffield Wednesday at home to Bolton Wanderers, winning 3-0. In total, he won 33 England caps.

13. Peter Phillip Bonetti

A goalkeeper who played for Chelsea away at Blackpool, winning 5-1, but injured his hand in the return fixture, which cost him a few games. He was capped seven times for England, including the 1970 quarter-final against West Germany. Passed away in April 2020.

14. James Christopher Armfield

He was with Blackpool in season 1963/64 – in fact, all of his career – but he missed the Boxing Day fixture versus Chelsea with an injury. Armfield served England and the sport well over 65 years as a player, manager and broadcaster. He was capped 43 times as a right-back.

15. Gerald Byrne

Byrne missed the Boxing Day visit of Stoke City with an injury but played in the return fixture in April. Another one-club man, Byrne served Liverpool FC as a left-back for 16 years, winning two caps for England in the same position.

17. Ronald Flowers

He played for Wolves on Boxing Day 1963, drawing 3-3 with Aston Villa, and served Wolves for 15 years as a midfield player, winning 49 caps for England.

18. Norman Hunter

Hunter was playing, and winning promotion, with Second Division Leeds United in season 1963/64. By the time he retired from football Hunter had won 28 caps for England as a tenacious defender. Passed away in April 2020.

19. Terence Lionel Paine

He played for Southampton in season 1963/64, who were in the Second Division at the time. Paine won 19 international caps for England as a winger, amassing a huge 919 career club games, including 824 in the league.

20. Ian Robert Callaghan

He played for Liverpool in their Boxing Day 6-1 victory over Stoke City. Liverpool's record appearance holder, he was capped four times by England as a winger.

22. George Edward Eastham

He was an Arsenal player in 1963/64 and thus did not play on Boxing Day 1963; however, he played two days later at Birmingham. He was capped 19 times for England.

———

The building of the squad was made more difficult by the fact that, as hosts, England did not have to qualify and the manager would have to try players and formations in home-nations fixtures and in friendlies, which was not ideal. We can see from the above selections that even as the tournament approached, Ramsey was still willing to try different players with minor tactical variances and this flexibility was certainly a factor in England's success – e.g. Geoff Hurst, whose first cap only came in early 1966.

In fact, the team who played together in the World Cup Final had only played as a starting XI for England six times – and three of those games were in the tournament. It is also worth repeating that all 11 players that day played outside the First Division at some stage in their careers. Of the 22-player squad who represented England in the most important World Cup in the country's history (still):

- 14 played for their First Division clubs on Boxing Day 1963

- three missed their fixture with injury

- one did not play due to his club not playing that day

- four were with Second Division clubs in 1963/64

Chapter 14

Summary & Conclusions

So, a wonderful day of football in the First Division with a diverse supporting cast of interesting characters covering some of the best players of this, or any other, era came to an end. Many football historians regard the early 60s as a golden age for football, before economic and commercial factors began to reveal what they would consider to be their ugly head.

Perhaps this was the last era when attackers had the better of defenders, as improved defensive discipline and structures took hold, making defending a coachable art form, which I guess developed from 1965 onwards, as evidenced by the World Cup-winning team of 1966 – Sir Alf Ramsey's 'Wingless Wonders'. There is a saying in football that attacking players win you fixtures but defenders win you championships, and perhaps that mentality developed from this era.

From this point, too, European football would begin to affect tactics and team set-up – Spurs had won a European trophy the season before, and West Ham would win another the following season – and it would be just five years before Manchester United would win the European Cup in 1968. English clubs dominated in Europe through the 70s and early 80s, before the European ban on the back of the tragedy at Heysel stopped that momentum.

Match of the Day was still about 12 months away from taking shape as a weekly programme and it developed a mass audience after its switch from the then wasteland of BBC2 – and the press and media exposure of the sport expanded rapidly from that point, assisted, of course, by England's World Cup win in 1966 on home soil.

These were days when the game was very much for the people and the players were paid not so very much more than the average skilled worker – many of the players travelled to the fixtures on the same transport as the fans, they just went in a different gate when they arrived at the ground.

Before the 'cult of the celebrity', the players lived in similar terrace housing and were often seen in the same locations – on trains, in snooker halls, pubs and clubs, and restaurants and – as we have seen on the way through the story – the drinking culture at many of the clubs was still very prevalent and as a result some of the players did not always look after themselves as well as they might. It was to be several more eras before players realised that they were multi-million pound assets to a business and acted accordingly and they were able to extend their careers for individual financial benefit.

Having said that, it was still a massively enjoyable era in our national sport and some would argue more enjoyable than the sanitised current era – there was generally little incentive to move clubs as wages were mostly on a par so players stayed much longer and the financial rewards were much less of an issue. However, with the abolition of the maximum wage in 1961 the initial knockings of wage inflation were perhaps stirring a tad and the lot of the players was starting to change from this point onwards – slowly at first.

It has been noticeable researching in detail some of the main characters that injuries were much more of an issue than in future years – what we regard as simple, treatable injuries now were often career threatening in the early 60s, and in an era before substitutions players were often sent back on the field of play when they perhaps should not have been. Pastoral care of the players was not a priority for the clubs and training sessions often involved a lot of running – reference the West Bromwich dispute with their manager when players were just starting to realise that to be successful you needed to be more savvy and tactical and they started to voice their opinion on such matters – a new breed of more enlightened player was starting to slowly emerge.

It is also surprising how many players' careers were effectively over by the time they reached 30, which I suspect is for three reasons:

1) The majority of the players did not care for their bodies, and poor diet and excessive alcohol consumption eventually caught up with them.

2) The late and haphazard treatment of injuries was often not in the players' best interests.

3) The physicality of the era on awful pitches eventually told on players' physiques and stamina.

The players played in very basic stadia by modern standards, and this was not to change until the late 80s and early 90s after the disaster at Hillsborough and issues elsewhere led to the Lord Justice Taylor Report recommending all-seater stadia, and developing income streams from Premier League broadcasting contracts allowed clubs to invest in new facilities, enabling them to attract a more discerning corporate clientele from the mid-90s onward.

Thankfully, a serious blight of English football had not really reared its head at this point. Hooliganism was one of the not-so-welcome manifestations of the new early 1960s freedoms we discussed earlier and it blighted our national sport for 20 years or more from the late 60s until all-seater stadia, cameras, better policing and intelligence brought it under some degree of control by the early 90s – at least in the grounds.

At this point – Boxing Day 1963 – I was seven years old but my father would not let me go with him to fixtures – but less than two years later I was a committed regular fan of the sport in general and Leicester City in particular. I am forever in debt to my father – Bill Davidson – for igniting my love for football, and sadly, but somehow fittingly, the last time I saw him was at Filbert Street in February 2002 before he passed the following week after being involved in a car crash.

Watching football in the mid-60s has stayed with me forever; the stark brick walls of the enclosures, the touch and smell of the mint condition programmes, the peeling posters on the walls, the aroma of stale onions, the beery smell of many of the patrons, the passing of small children to the front and the cutting edge humour and 'advice' to the players, along with the banter.

All the fixtures started at 3pm on a Saturday, with most finishing by 4.40pm on the dot, allowing you to race to the nearest newsagent that sold sports specials to check where that day's result had left your favourite team in the table.

All of which are now long gone – in many cases thankfully – but it was an era that began to change our football heritage and our social history forever, but we should never forget the impact pre-Premiership eras had in the development of the sport we all love so dearly.

Bibliography

Belton, Brian, *Burn Budgie Byrne* (Breedon Books, 2004)

White, Alex, *The Men Who Made Fulham FC* (Tempus Publishing, 2002)

Jackman, Mike, *Blackburn Rovers – The Complete Record* (Breedon Books, 2009)

Smith, Dave and Paul Taylor, *Of Fossils & Foxes – Official History of Leicester City* (Polar Publishing, 1989)

McLintock, Frank, *True Grit* (Headline Books, 2005)

Morgan, Willie, *On the Wing* (Sport Media, 2013)

Barnard, Rob, *The Jimmy Hagan Story* (History Press, 2007)

Crooks, Richard, *Grandad What Was Football like in the 1960s?* (Pitch Publishing, 2015)

Crawford, Ray, *Curse of the Jungle Boy* (PB Publishing, 2007)

A Portrait of Stoke City FC in the 1960s & 1970s (Sentinel Papers)

Tottenham Hotspur FC Archive – courtesy John Fennelly

West Ham FC Archive – courtesy *They Fly So High* – Steve Marsh

Aston Villa FC Archive – courtesy Rob Bishop

Burnley FC Archive – courtesy Shaun Borman

Leicester City Match Details – courtesy Dave Smith

Sheffield Telegraph Archive

British Newspaper Archive

Acknowledgements

Thank you to Martin Tyler for very kindly writing the foreword. Making his commentary debut in 1974, Martin is a true legend of the game, and I am humbled by his kindness.

Many thanks to my friend Steve Jacques, whose design expertise and patience knows no bounds. You are a constant inspiration to me and the fact that you have collaborated with me now on two books is a source of amazement to me.

Bizarrely, thanks to my wife Sue who is as uninterested in football as it is possible to be. She saw me struggling with coming up with a title for this book whilst she was listening to her favourite band The Four Seasons and came up with an inspired choice – bravo!

Thanks to all the club historians who answered my requests for information – your patience was much appreciated. They – like me – have a strong desire to maintain each club's heritage for future generations. Football was not always new and shiny with a staff of 20 on team benches – in the early 60s it was sometimes two, with one having a bucket and sponge.

Thanks are due to the lecturers (Doctor Carter and Professor Polley) at the International Centre for Sports History and Culture at De Montfort University here in Leicester, who have instilled in me the requirement to do proper research in any historical work – your patience with me has been appreciated.

A massive retrospective thank you to the players and managers who entertained us so royally on that Boxing Day all those years ago. I hope I have reflected the era in which you played – the good bits and the not so good bits. You all made a contribution to one of the most memorable days in the rich history of league football in England, which dates back to 1888.

Finally, a thank you to all the readers of this book – I hope you have enjoyed reading about these fixtures and the assembly of characters who combined to give a rich narrative to events.

Also available at all good book stores

9781785316524

9781785316463

9781785316906

9781785316654

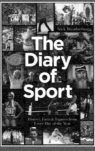

9781785316289

9781785316531

9781785316548

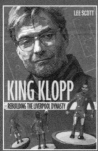

9781785316500

9781785316791

WEST HAM UNITED

BLACKBURN ROVERS

FOOTBALL LEAGUE—Division One

THURSDAY 26th DECEMBER 1963 at 11 a.m.

No. 31

The Directors, Players and Staff

of the West Ham United Football Club

extend Heartiest Seasonal Greetings

to all their Friends in the Realm of

Soccer both "at Home and Away"

OFFICIAL PROGRAMME

6d

Helliar & Sons, London, E.13

NIGHTMARE AT U PARK

tional re

The p
the poo
dogged
mers'
half.

Peter

WEST HAM UTD. 2
BLACKBURN R. 8

THERE was a distinct air of faint bewilderment about the Blackburn players at the end of this fantastic Boxing Day pantomime at Upton Park. One or two grabbed each other's hands in extra firm grips . . . almost as if to make sure that it had all really happened and that they were not soon to awake from the storied sleep which all too frequently follows Christmas Day's feasting. The match certainly had all the qualities of a dream for

disaster made it difficult later to get the course of the game in true perspective. The facts are, however, that it was an affair of two very separate phases, neatly divided by the interval.

THE FORTUNE

elusive
day, al
any ev
of the
appear
with th
Fred
lethal
tions.
On
dismal

PRICE

6d